Betsy Scassero

A TIME TO HEAL

A TIME TO HEAL

The story of a healer

by

GORDON TURNER

Best wishes
Gordon Turner

London
TALMY, FRANKLIN

First Published in Great Britain 1974
By Talmy, Franklin Limited
124 Knightsbridge
London SW1X 7PE

ISBN 0 900735 29 5

Design/computer composition/print in England by
Eyre & Spottiswoode Ltd at Grosvenor Press

FOR
DAPHNE AND SHADOW

A Time to kill, and a Time to Heal; a Time
to break down, and a Time to build up;
A Time to weep, and a Time to laugh; a Time
to mourn, and a Time to dance . . .

Ecclesiastes iii - 3 & 4

PREFACE
BY SHEL TALMY

I first met Gordon Turner for professional reasons in the Autumn of 1964. My wife had given birth to twins the previous March and had subsequently developed a very rare post-natal condition. She had begun to lose feeling in her extremities. She was unable to hold objects without dropping them and would stumble while walking.

The three medical specialists we consulted all concurred in their diagnosis; disseminated sclerosis. When asked about treatment, I was told that there was none, and that the disease was progressively degenerative and incurable. My wife would eventually be in a state of total paralysis, until such time as it reached her heart.

About a week after hearing this cheery prognosis, I was pouring out the problem to a friend, who commiserated with me and eventually made a suggestion. He had heard of a healer named Gordon Turner, who was apparently doing miraculous things. Acting on my basic philosophy of trying almost everything once, I took my wife to see him. Being a sceptic, I decided not to tell Gordon what the specialists had said, but only that she had lost the feeling in her hands and feet. This was a fairly easy thing to do, as my wife hadn't been told the real reason for the disability. She was under the impression that it was a nervous condition.

Gordon came out after a ten minute examination, and told me in private that he was in no doubt that she had developed disseminated sclerosis and, what was far more important, that he thought he could cure it.

To cut a long story short, he was as good as his word. In two months of weekly treatments she had regained all

1

sensation and was pronounced completely cured.

Nine years further on, as of this moment, she is still perfectly well.

I don't confess to know how Gordon is able to accomplish these cures; suffice it to say that they are accomplished.

Gordon himself does not know how it is done. He has intensely researched the reasons without obtaining any concrete solutions. I don't think it's based on faith, as many of his successes have been with very young children and animals. Gordon has a gift, and it's fortunate for those of us who have been the beneficiaries, that he decided to use it.

This autobiography of Gordon Turner's is only the tip of the iceberg. I have a feeling that if Gordon decided to recount all of his adventures, they would make up a twenty volume set. At the time of writing I think I have convinced him to start on volume two.

London
December 1973

PROLOGUE

Death is something which happens to other people. We may pretend to accept its reality, but deep down inside we know that we are different. Several million years of evolution, twenty thousand years of religion and seven thousand years of science have only served to immunise us from the obvious. For us, life — at least in our current identity — is on strictly leasehold terms. But we strut about in the guise of freeholders. In our arrogance, we retain the ability to be surprised constantly at each repetition of natural law. This last vestige of innocence is possibly our most endearing quality.

The vast majority of human activities are gigantic self-deceptions. We gather wealth or possessions as a death prophylaxis. We worship gods created in our own image. We build, organise, administrate, cultivate, create and procreate. Eternity engulfs all as the incoming tide washes away children's sand castles. From our first strangulated post-foetal breath there is only one certainty — impermanence.

Change is the first basic reality. Suns and planets: solar systems and galaxies: oceans and continents: forests and deserts: mountains and plains: ants and men: for all it is the same law — constant change.

Through it all there is a rhythm. As the super-stars, quasars and pulsars beat out the pulse of the universe across the immensity of space, so the heart, that tiny human pump, counts our seconds in eternity. Pump — pause — pump — pause: inhale — exhale: night — day — light — dark: spring — autumn: summer — winter: life — death — life: thus even the grim reaper is reduced to a momentary hesitation between life and life.

3

Chapter I

At twenty-five minutes past five on the afternoon of Wednesday, the 28th September 1966 I felt a sudden loss of mobility in my left hand. Ironically, I was attempting to heal an elderly man suffering from the after-effects of a stroke. I asked him to excuse me and left the room. My left leg dragged and my speech was slurred.

I had been aware for several months that my blood pressure was too high. I should have gone to hospital for tests, but there was so much to do. I was Chairman of the Healers' Federation — a national body I had helped to found — and administrative difficulties made it imperative that I be available constantly.

Then there was the annual Summer School for Healers — another of my brain children — which had ended only a couple of days before. How could I possibly have missed it? Then there were my patients — who could possibly look after them?

At twenty-five minutes past five I was totally indispensable. At twenty-six minutes past five on the same afternoon I was effectively dispensed with. Just like that! All it took was one little cerebral thrombus. One little blood vessel, which could not stand up to the unreasonable pressures to which it had for so long been subjected, brought my life's work crashing about my feet like so much powdered plaster.

An exasperated friend once described me as a cross between Mr. Micawber and an ostrich. When in doubt, I tend to bury my head in the sand and hold fast to the proposition that 'something must inevitably turn up'. Certainly, on this occasion, the assessment was accurate. I struggled into bed and waited for the symptoms to go away. In the event they did not oblige.

Two hours later paralysis had developed so far that one side of my body was totally immobilised and my speech was rapidly deteriorating. It occurred to me, for the first time, that I might be dying. The implications were so momentous that my mind refused to grasp them. I wanted to make a gesture, cock-a-snook at fate. All I could think of was to send out for champagne. By this time, however, I was far too ill to enjoy it.

Part of my mind was crystal clear; concentrated and yet remote, as if viewing all that took place through the wrong end of binoculars. The immediate foreground of my mind was confused. My memory had difficulty in placing events in their correct chronological pattern. If I was called upon to communicate directly, I became overwhelmed with emotion. I later learned that my cerebral disturbance had occurred in an area of the brain which closely involved the emotions.

Although I did not realise it at the time, my mind was operating in a manner with which I was quite unfamiliar. It was as if the barriers dividing the separate compartments had dissolved. Random thoughts emerged in company with un-related ideas, each complementing the other in a fresh or unique way. Rigid preconceptions which I had been unable to recognise were immediately, almost ridiculously, obvious. And all of this was happening spontaneously. Mind ceased to be a tool requiring discipline and training. It was a landscape in which one might wander and never fail to be diverted.

My doctor examined me. He confirmed what I thought. I had had a stroke. Within the hour, he brought in a consultant. They wanted me to go into hospital immediately. I managed to ask them whether I was dying. They tried to avoid the question. When I insisted, they admitted that my condition was grave. I decided that if I was dying I would far rather do it in my own bed at home. When they saw I was adamant they left. All that remained of the night was eternity.

There followed a kind of dialogue within my mind. The experience was so vivid that the voices were distinct and seemed perfectly audible. Each conscious thought was immediately voiced. After a slight delay, answering words would echo within my head. Often they would seem unrelated to my thought; but at times it was not unlike holding a long distance telephone conversation.

At some point — it is impossible to fix this experience precisely in time — another part of my mind provided a visual rationalisation. I saw myself, as from a great distance, lying beneath a large cone of spinning particles of golden light.

There was a curious sense of detachment from the prone figure. Somehow, I knew that the cone was the configuration of all the different aspects of my being. The physical form was no more than one dimly glowing ember in a furnace of energy. The 'answering voice' seemed to emanate from the cone. The dialogue went something like this:

·"So this is it. I'm dying."

"Unimportant."

"There are so many things I wanted to do. I've wasted so much time. So many places I wanted to see. . . ."

"All relative to time."

"It means leaving behind all I hold dear."

"Relative to motive."

I could not see how friendship and personal relationships could be relative to motives. It seemed desperately cruel that I should have to face separation from those I loved. Even as I shaped thoughts of protestation they were swamped by what seemed an even more awful realisation. Life as I had known it would continue, but without me.

"Self pity."

What else was there but life viewed through self? At the time, I held as a basic tenet of faith, utter conviction in the survival of personality after physical death. This was a corner stone of the foundations upon which I had tried to construct

6

my life.

"Self and personality?"

I could cope with this. I had given a lot of thought to the problem of identity. I believed in an indestructible spirit. This was inextinguishable — even by death. It was this realisation of man's spiritual nature which had given rise to all the world's great religions. In the face of death, I refused to give way to nihilism.

A cry from the Egyptian Book of the Dead, which has survived the milleniums, came into my mind. When the heart of the deceased is weighed in the Great Balance by Anubis against an ostrich feather, and he is at last led before his judges Osiris and Horus, he prays, "Let me remember then the name I bore!" I tried shaping my name as if it were a charm to which I might cling.

"Gordon Turner, born on April 1st with the sun in Aries. I am a healer. For more than twenty years this has been my life."

These were points of positive identification. I had a name which was my own, a birthday which was mine and a vocation. These at least must survive.

And so the dialogue continued along similar lines. At first as a battle to preserve life in its present form. Gradually, point by point, accepting the greater reality of change.

It is difficult, thinking back over this period, to arrange time in its usual perspective. There must have been fairly long lapses of normal consciousness during which I was in coma. In fact, it was the evening of the following day that they at last persuaded me to go into hospital. The argument which finally won me round was that dying at home tends to impose unpleasant social complications on those who have to clear things up.

It has been said that a drowning man sees his entire life pass before him in the space of a few seconds. My own experience ranged more freely in time. It was an exercise in perspective.

7

Certainly, I experienced vivid recall of certain periods of my life — so much so, that at the time I believed myself to be reliving the events.

Frequently, such recall was followed by mental protestations in which I again felt myself involved in a dialogue, which, in turn, seemed to provide some form of catharsis. It was as if various periods of my life, which had settled into separate pools, were released to flow into the central reservoir of my being. There was neither good nor ill: right nor wrong: only absolute unity.

Before the ambulance arrived to take me to hospital, I managed to convey to an old friend my wishes concerning my few worldly possessions. They were a small burden, shed without any deep feelings of loss or regret. In any case, I no longer felt the physical world to be real. It was part of a dream from which I was in the process of waking.

As the stretcher was carried out, my little brown mongrel bitch tried to jump onto it with me (she was then fifteen years old and died five years later at the wonderful age of twenty). This tested my emotions to the limit. But I had developed a deep inner peace. I was ready to die — possibly even looking forward to it.

To arrive at a large London teaching hospital as an emergency casualty is a pretty traumatic experience at any time; to do so when you are as ill as I was is shattering. Some hospitals should be reserved for those who are sufficiently well to fend off their ministrations.

The consultant had assured me, before I left home, that he had advised the hospital of my condition and supplied them with any particulars they might need, so that I might be spared the ordeal of a lengthy examination. By this time, my speech was a very real problem, so I was naturally grateful that I would not have to struggle to answer a great many questions.

The journey from a couch in Casualty to a bed temporarily

squeezed into an already overcrowded ward took more than two hours. The consultant's efforts to smooth my passage had presumably fallen on stony ground. I hope that I may never again feel as I did that night. I had faced up to death — and even the possibility of total extinction; but to be permanently paralysed, the helpless victim of such a system — before the prospect of that fate the imagination quailed.

The young doctor who had questioned me at such length in Casualty arrived to see me safely installed. Presumably, it having at last dawned upon him that I found it extremely difficult to speak, he further deduced that all my mental faculties were similarly impaired.

"He'll be off our hands by tomorrow," he told a nurse. "Tell Staff not to allow anybody to take that bed away. We may need it." Apparently as an afterthought he added, "Oh, when you think he is on the way out, let me know." He vanished from my field of vision, suffused by his aura of pompous authority.

Heavy sedation afforded me temporary nirvana. I came to with the feeling of floating just above my body. There was a momentary sensation of blissful freedom. And then, as full consciousness returned, I was fighting to breathe. In — out: in — out: I existed for the space of each laboured gasp of air.

The doctor's voice caused me to notice that the curtains had been pulled round my bed. A nurse was sitting beside me holding an oxygen mask over my face. They were engrossed in a whispered conversation.

"What about Friday?"

"Shhh!" she hissed.

"Come on! Give me a definite answer."

"I'm supposed to be on duty."

"Go on. Sister will let you find a replacement."

"Not her . . ." She broke off as she noticed me looking at her. "I think he's conscious."

"Blast!"

He started to examine me casually and rather roughly. I took another breath and summoned up as much strength as I could command. With an effort I pulled my face away from the oxygen mask.

"Don't bother," I gasped. "I'll be better tomorrow and then I can see a real doctor." It even sounded like my own voice. I was going to live.

Daylight found the curtains removed from round my bed. I was breathing more easily but the paralysis was just as bad. I tested my leg and arm for muscular response and on the basis of the slight movement which remained, set myself a programme of exercises to be undertaken every half hour. The next thing was to resume command of my own circumstances.

Sister bore patiently with my laboured speech. She made several telephone calls for me and even held the receiver while I spoke to my secretary. Within a comparatively short time I was being transferred to the private wing of the hospital.

British hospitals tend to subscribe to a policy which may best be summed up as a conspiracy of silence. What this amounts to is — 'leave it all to us, we know best'. I refused to accept this and insisted on an honest summary of my condition. It was not very encouraging.

I had rallied remarkably from heart failure; but they still feared that this might recur. There remained a very real danger of a further stroke. It was impossible to predict the future if I did survive. The paralysis was extensive. I might spend the remainder of my life a helpless cripple.

I dared to hope. After all, as a healer I had seen recovery from what seemed to be terminal illnesses. If death came, I could now meet it as a friend. But having resolved to fight I would put up as good an effort as I possibly could. Being careful not to overtax my strength, I gently encouraged my useless limbs back to life.

The private ward I now occupied had three beds. One of these was empty and the other was occupied by an Irish engineer. He was as tough as old boots and perfect company for me in my present frame of mind. He helped me bribe a porter to hold me upright so that I might try to exercise my legs.

I dragged myself back into the world with the greatest effort of will I had ever been called upon to exert. I accepted such medication as the hospital was able to offer; but I was never in any doubt. If I was to get better, it was up to me.

In the long hours which had followed the onset of my illness I had passed through my wilderness. I felt, it was hard to analyse, in some way changed. It was not bravado, but something more, which now caused me to treat my paralysis as a huge joke. This was an attitude in which my Irish ward companion was all too ready to join. Between us we managed to disrupt the institutionalising elements of hospital life to our own immense satisfaction.

One battle I had was for sufficient help to get me into a 'proper' bath. On the fourth day I emerged victorious. Between a porter and a frail nurse I slithered my feet along the corridor to the bathroom. Just before they lowered me into the benison of warm water, I caught a glimpse of myself in the mirror. It shocked me. Beneath a stubble of beard the muscles of my face had collapsed, lowering one eye and dragging down the side of my mouth. I looked terrible. Somehow, I still managed to sustain the joke.

By the eighth day, I could balance on my own feet with the aid of a stick in my right hand. How I hated that stick — it was a symbol of failure. A young physiotherapist, in an effort to be helpful, brought me a leg iron to try. It was only the good-humoured restraining influence of my Irish friend which prevented me from hitting her with it.

Shortly after the war, I belonged to a golf club where a legless air ace used to play. If you were in front of him, however fast you might walk, he was forever hitting his ball into your game and hustling to come through. He was a national hero and the subject of much admiration; but occasionally his aggressive impatience used to irritate me. Now, I was rapidly learning that the disabled have to fight if they are to survive on equal terms with the fit.

I asked for the hospital barber to visit me. He was a lugubrious little man who complained constantly. After a brain episode such as mine, the face is ultra-sensitive. His scraping and scratching caused me considerable discomfort.

"Haven't you another razor?" I pleaded.

"I keep the other one for cadavers," he explained. "It's my best."

"Well, surely you can go a bit easy on my face," I protested. "You must know how to shave someone better than that."

He drew himself up to his full five feet four inches. "It ain't my fault, Sir. I don't get much call 'ere to shave faces."

For the first time it dawned upon me that the duties of a surgical barber are somewhat different from those of his more conventional colleagues.

I discharged myself from the hospital on the tenth day. They advised me that they thought my decision foolish, but I was adamant. They offered me an ambulance to take me home. I refused and asked for a taxi. At my request, the driver took me through Hyde Park and stopped for a few minutes beside the Serpentine.

Everything appeared fresh and new. I saw the trees as if for the first time. I laughed like a delighted child at the antics of the ducks. With assistance, I left the car and stood for a moment on the grass. It was moist and springy beneath my feet. Physical life might be leasehold, but it was good!

Safely at home in my own bed, my little brown mongrel bitch jumped up beside me, gathered my paralysed arm between her paws and as she licked it gently, she whimpered.

12

I wept. But mine were tears of victory. I was not to know that the real battle had scarcely started.

Chapter II

"It's a matter of taking things very quietly. In time, you may be able to walk as far as the top of the road. But you've got to face up to it, there are a great many things you will never be able to do again. It will be like living with one dimension missing."

My doctor at that time was a German. He was a quiet, thorough person. He was aware that I was a healer; but always studiously referred to my work as psychotherapy. After he left, I tried to analyse what he meant by 'living with one dimension missing'.

I had been at home for about a month and it was becoming increasingly obvious that I was very badly handi-capped.

True, there were areas in which I had made excellent progress. My speech was infinitely better. The muscles of my face were splendidly improved. With the aid of a stick I could walk indoors for very short distances without assistance. But there were new problems to be faced.

Large areas of my memory appeared to be obliterated. My normal vocabulary was much reduced. People visited me who were old friends and yet, to me, they seemed perfect strangers. This proved embarrassing, as my public work — lectures, research, administration, etc. — naturally caused me to have a wide circle of acquaintances. I started to dread and avoid callers.

Worse, I was having blackouts which were almost certainly caused by brain damage. They came without warning. On one frightful day I had no less than twenty-nine. The falls were smothering me with bruises and they were undermining what confidence I had left. Pills, prescribed to ameliorate this, were drugs whose effects I found confusing and distressing. I preferred to put up with the blackouts; even though they persisted throughout the nights as well as the days.

Since my stroke, I had been having recurrent nightmares. They were extremely vivid and usually involved drowning or smothering. These were not difficult to interpret. Brain disturbances leave the nerve endings ultra-sensitive. Even the weight of bedclothes can become unbearably restrictive.

Perhaps the worst problem of all was my feeling of utter uselessness. I had been accustomed to a very full and active life. It was difficult, especially with my paralysed arm, which showed little or no progress thus far, to envisage a time in the future when I might return to my full-time work as a healer. All in all, I felt considerably less of a victor than when I had first returned home from hospital.

I lay on my bed and looked through the large studio window at the leaves on the poplars. They were changing colour and one or two drifted to earth with the breeze. It would be a long winter looking at those bare trees. Would the spring find me still lying there wistfully watching until the fresh green buds became leaves in their turn?

"Damn!"

I was giving way to self pity. I forced myself to stand up and dragged my way across to the door. I lifted my limp paralysed hand onto the handle and tried to grip. It was still beyond me − but one day soon . . . That was the answer. I must stick to the struggle of the present moment. I made my laborious journey back to the bed and lay there sweating and exhausted. I would turn that handle! It might take forever, but I would do it!

Over the next few weeks I started to face up to the implications of my 'missing dimension'. I wrote to the Healers' Federation and told them that I would not be able to allow my name to be put forward as Chairman at the forthcoming elections or continue to organise their Summer

Schools. I had been associated with the Federation since its inception; but I am not really a committee man. At heart I am a rebel. I was amazed at how little regret I felt at shedding these burdens.

At the same time, I resigned every other committee and organisational appointment I held. Another rather sadder task was arranging for my healing work to be taken over by others. At last all was completed and my telephone stopped ringing. It was a salutary lesson which we all have to learn: we are not indispensable.

For the first time in many years I had time and enough to think. I read, exercised my paralysed limbs and meditated. Life had been so frenetic that I had not realised my soul had been unable to catch up with my body.

I was desperately hard up and therefore, when a radio play I had written as a mental exercise to help my vocabulary, immediately after my stroke, was accepted by the B.B.C., it was a double triumph. Not only had my first attempt met with success, but it opened up a possible source of income which I badly needed.

Christmas 1966 was happy and peaceful. I shall long remember it for the companionship and support of dear and loving friends. I looked towards the New Year with mixed feelings. There was so much to be thankful for and yet there was so much that I desperately missed.

On New Year's Eve I had an intensely lucid dream which impressed me out of all proportion to its importance.

I was walking through a dark forest. My left arm was strapped to my left leg which had a lead weight chained to the ankle. It was imperative that I get through the forest as quickly as possible; but the effort of dragging my left side was too much for me.

I tried to pick up the lead weight with my right hand, but it was too heavy for me to lift. In trying, I fell into a deep hollow which was filled with dead leaves. However hard I tried, at each attempt to climb out, the weight dragged me back deeper than ever. Utterly exhausted, I shouted:

"I can't do it on my own!"

R., a man with whom I had at one time worked closely but who I felt had treated me rather badly when my health had failed, appeared at the crest of the hollow.

"Charge it up to the angels, old chap," he called down to me.

"You're an unctuous old hypocrite!" I retorted.

"But it says so in the Bible," said R.

"And it says a lot of other silly things as well," I replied, exasperated.

"Why don't you fly out of there?" R. asked.

In the context of the dream this seemed an eminently sensible suggestion.

"How?" I asked.

"Wait for the sun to come out and then hop on one leg," R. told me.

At that moment the sun appeared in bright shafts of light between the trees. Obediently I hopped up and down. Sure enough, the weight fell off and I was soaring above the forest in an ecstasy of flight.

I woke up full of hope and immediately tried to move my arm. I was surprised to find it still paralysed. So vivid had the dream seemed that I wrote it down in my daybook so that I should not forget it.

A couple of days later I received a letter from R. In it he asked my forgiveness if he had seemed to lack understanding when I was first ill. He was unwell himself and my illness had subsequently been much on his mind.

He went on to say: "I know you must feel as if your arms are tied and you have been burdened with worry. Remember we are taught, 'He has given His angels charge over us'. Only remember this and you will transcend all your troubles. Look to the light and keep your faith and you will rise to even greater heights."

R. really had been very unkind to me. It was an unworthy thought but it leapt instantly to my mind:

"The unctuous old hypocrite." At once the letter and dream came together. I looked at the date. It had been posted before my dream.

I was quite sure that I had not been thinking about R. If someone hurts me sufficiently, my ostrich characteristic takes over. My head goes firmly into the sand until I have completely forgotten his existence. This was the case with R.

Presumably, the dream had been clairvoyant rather than precognitive. Some part of me must have been aware of the contents of the letter before it arrived. Although it was quite unexpected, there was nothing remarkable about it as a communication. The wording was fairly typical of the sender. Could it have been that I had, somehow, telepathically intercepted R.'s thoughts? If this were the case it might explain why the words had been reproduced in so garbled a form in the dream.

I thought a lot about this dream. It intrigued me. The experience had been so vivid and the subsequent outcome fascinating. And yet nothing really significant had emerged. My recent experiences had made me ultra-conscious of my 'inner' life. I determined to try to be more conscious of my dreams. For this purpose, I would keep paper and pencil beside my bed so that I might make notes before each dream was forgotten.

Being a prolific dreamer I naturally expected to gather plenty of material. It was a washout. For five nights in succession I was restless, frequently having to sit up in a chair because of protracted bouts of pain in my paralysed side. The odd scraps I was able to record were all too obviously the flotsam and jetsam of my subconscious mind.

The first 'different' dream nearly slipped through my defences without being noted. In the strictest sense it was

18

questionable whether it was a dream so much as a fleeting subconscious impression.

For some years, I had been supplying copies of my book *An Outline of Spiritual Healing* to patients and other interested people who sent their orders to me postally. The book was temporarily out of print and consequently copies were strictly limited.

I awoke feeling intensely irritated. There was something important which should have been done but had been overlooked. My memory refused to supply the relevant information and I put this down to brain damage. This increased my irritation.

Suddenly it came to my mind with graphic clarity. That was it. We had received a cheque from Australia for six books. The cheque was for £8. 17s. (pre-decimalised sterling) and this did not coincide with the correct value of the order. I could not remember exactly when it had arrived, but I was sure it must have been within the last couple of weeks. My secretary must have put it to one side either because of our low stock or because of the discrepancy between the cheque and the cost of the books. I would tackle her about it as soon as she arrived.

I became so agitated about this Australian cheque that I struggled along the corridor and started to hunt for it among my office files. There was no record of it anywhere. When I taxed my secretary about it, she was unable to recall the order and joined me in my search. It was nowhere to be found.

The next morning I received a cheque from Australia for £8. 17s. It was for six copies of my book, the surplus to cover airmail postage. The sender was anxious to receive the books as soon as possible as one of them was to be a birthday present.

Unfortunately the letter had been delayed in the post. It was dated two weeks prior to its arrival. There was no chance that the books could arrive in time for the birthday.

In fact, the amount was still wrong when set against postage. To the best of my recollection I had never before received a cheque for this amount from Australia and I certainly have not done so since.

This dream, or, to be more accurate, cognition, had certain points of similarity with the first. They both involved letters which were in transit at the time of my experience. They both seemed to involve clairvoyance rather than pre-cognition, and in each case there might have been mental agitation on the part of the sender. In R.'s case, because my illness was on his mind. In the case of the Australian cheque, because one of the books was required urgently.

It seemed to me that the second 'dream' varied from the first in two important respects. It was accurately sensed, even to the precise amount of the cheque, and was a 'wake' impression rather than a dream recollection. Presumably this might account for its greater precision. The subconscious mind may embroider dreams as we attempt to remember them in detail.

Over the years I had had a great many dreams which seemed to be clairvoyant or precognitive. The dreams about R. and the Australian cheque coming so close together put an idea into my head.

Perhaps my doctor was wrong, after all. Maybe there was no need for there to be a missing dimension. Indeed, this might be the perfect opportunity to open new dimensions of consciousness.

The whole pattern of my life had been affected by inner gifts and senses which did not seem to be possessed by everyone. This prolonged period of inactivity might provide the perfect opportunity to examine these 'gifts' and relate them to the not uneventful course my life had taken.

I was not shut off. My inner life remained as real as ever. The dreams served to remind me of my inner gifts.

I looked once more at the poplars through my bedroom window. They were now stripped bare of leaves by the winter winds, and seemed to nod their tall heads in agreement. I could still become an explorer in a world where my physical limitations would not hold me back. After all, had not my life thus far been an adventure in two worlds?

Chapter III

People often ask me how exactly I describe myself. I reply, "A healer." Invariably, there is a supplementary question.

"Yes, but what sort of healer? Are you a faith healer, a spiritual healer or what?"

"Just a plain healer, without any form of prefix," I say.

It seldom satisfies them. Not that I mind: it would not have satisfied me fifteen years ago.

When we are young, labels seem terribly important. One has to have them for everything. I have gathered as many as the next man in my time. In one passionate year I was severally a communist, socialist, atheist, liberal and young conservative. If I remember rightly it was in that same year that I went through Confirmation as a member of the Church of England. At the time, I had all the experience of sixteen years behind me.

For most of my life I have used the term 'spiritual healer'. And felt really passionate about it, too. If a newspaper mistakenly described me as a 'faith healer', I would put it down to their ignorance or prejudice and write a letter to the editor pointing out his mistake. Now, I do not much mind. I have a dear friend, one of whose favourite sayings is: "Never know your Vicar". This sums up in a nutshell my reasons for dropping the prefix 'spiritual'.

Spiritual healers are neither more nor less spiritual than any other cross-section of mankind. In fact, when gathered together in organisations, they can be a pretty hard lot. They tend to have strong convictions, which can make them more intransigent than most. Those who have the strongest pretensions to spirituality can be very tough cookies. I would rather mix it with wrestlers of my acquaintance than one lady noted for the high tone of her public prayers.

Healers, like people the world over, come in different shapes and sizes. Their opinions and ideas vary as they do among any group made up from a variety of backgrounds and circumstances. When patients get better they want to believe 'their' healer is a very 'spiritual' man.

Take my friend's advice: "Never know your Healer". That is, unless you are prepared to accept him as a perfectly ordinary person, just like yourself.

Most healers use the word 'spiritual' to signify that the treatment they give is of the 'spirit' rather than the 'flesh'. This does not stop them handing out breathing exercises and other mundane advice. No, I will stay with 'healer' without any other ramifications. There is time enough to get round to the label 'spiritual' when we are all sure we know what we are talking about by generally accepted definition.

I have a theory that we drift into most of our convictions — even some of those to which we later subscribe with the greatest passion. Our politics may swing about throughout our lives but most of us adapt like chameleons to the environment in which we feel most secure. There are not many real converts, either politically or religiously. The vast majority of people prefer to travel along lines of least resistance. When the going gets too tough, politicians and religious leaders are usually ready to adapt themselves to a changing situation. That is how God manages to be on both sides during a war.

I did not become a healer. When I think back, I realise that healing threads through the warp and woof of my life as far back as I am able to remember. To begin with it was injured birds and small wild creatures of every description. Our gardener taught me to breathe on them and ". . . love 'un well again." Even insects were the victims of my all too eager ministrations.

When the carp in a nearby pond developed a fungus

disease, my brother and I saved them from extinction by keeping as many as we could rescue in every conceivable container we could put our hands on. We 'doctored' the fungus with saltpetre and the few we cured were transferred to a clean pond about a mile away. Later, we restocked the diseased pond and a healthy colony of carp survive there to this day. At the time Geoffrey was nine and I was coming up for seven.

When I grew older, it was rugger injuries. I coped with my first dislocated shoulder before I was twelve. I did not know how I did it. Our gardener used to say: "Master Gordon's got green fingers". As far as I was concerned, if that was good enough for him then it was good enough for me. I had a greater respect for our old gardener than I had for any of my well-educated teachers at school.

Until I was fifteen I wanted to be a veterinary surgeon. In school vacations, whenever the opportunity presented itself, I would help on farms or at stables. I became a pretty good 'midwife'. I have assisted at the birth of most domestic animals. Although to date I have not helped a human baby into the world, since the principle is the same it should not be too daunting.

Shortly after my seventh birthday I was packed off to boarding school. Margate College in Kent was a marvellous school. Both my brothers were lucky enough to complete their education there. We wore royal blue shorts and blazers, an orange shirt with an open neck and orange-topped socks. Our garters displayed a coloured flash to denote which 'House' we were in. Mine were green, as were those of my brothers, which meant we were the proud supporters of a certain Mr. Caley, who maintained rigid discipline with the help of a long-handled clothes brush known to the boys as 'the tickler'.

At night we slept in long dormitories and listened to the mournful wail of ships' foghorns from across the Goodwin

Sands. The headmaster, Major Leach-Lewis, was an utterly just man. We were punished — by today's standards severely — but never unfairly. I have met many Old Margatonians since and they all remember the School with affectionate pride.

Alas, the Old School is no more. Its boys were scattered by evacuation at the outbreak of war, and German shells, lobbed at random across the English Channel, razed its buildings to the ground. Now it is a municipal car park. All that remains is a green door hanging on rusted hinges. Above it is a notice, almost indecipherable, bearing the words "Junior Boys".

I left Margate College before its unhappy end, having won a place at Berkhamsted — a Public School dating back to the reign of Henry VIII and the dissolution of the monasteries. Part of the old Monastery remains, wedged between the school's more modern buildings.

My mother had been dead for less than a month when I arrived at my new school. From the first day I hated it. The fagging system, now I believe abolished, lent itself to bullying. Where I had found Margate tough, I found Berkhamsted cruel. It was a case of absolute incompatibility. When we finally parted company, several years later, I felt as if I were being released from penal servitude.

By extraction, I inherit Celtic blood from both sides of my family. Our 'feyness', I am sure, comes from my mother. She was a diminutive woman, half an inch short of five feet, with deep, intense brown eyes. Despite her constant ill health, I remember her as always laughing.

Although she loved all animals passionately, she had a strange phobia about cats. If a cat were in a room she would sense it at once, even if it were out of sight. I can remember her having to leave a train because a cardboard box on the luggage rack contained a kitten. In the perverse way cats have, they would always come straight to her. Perhaps this phobia was prophetic. Her final illness was precipitated by

25

shock when a stray cat ran through the open doors of the french windows, into our lounge where mother was sitting, and jumped onto her lap.

Most of the surviving members of mother's family had emigrated to Canada. One morning there was a heated argument at the breakfast table. Mother had had a dream in which her brother Cyril, who was in Toronto, came to her and told her that he had died. She had spent the remainder of the night crying, to my father's intense irritation. When, in the morning, she insisted on wearing black, it was too much for poor father. The next letter we received from Canada confirmed mother's dream, even to the hour of my uncle's death.

I never met my maternal aunts and uncles. A veil was drawn over this side of the family which made me feel that there must be something vaguely scandalous.

A constant source of discord between my parents was my mother's brother Harry. As far as we children were concerned he was just a name, but we learned quite a lot about him. He persistently wrote to my father asking for money. He would not work and squandered every penny he could scrape together on his racing pigeons. I saw a photograph of him once. A chubby young man frozen in faded sepia, with a Lord Kitchener moustache and bulging watery eyes. Poor Uncle Harry, he did not look capable of so dreadful a 'vice' as racing pigeons.

After mother died, her cousin came down from the North to help my father in the days immediately preceding the funeral. My sister, Sylvia, and I saw her coming in the gate. She was so like my mother in appearance that for a frightful moment we thought there had been a mistake and mother was not dead after all.

We could not forgive her. A few days later we caught the poor woman trying on clothes from mother's wardrobe. We kicked up such a fuss that my father had to pack her off home without waiting until after the funeral. When one is suffering bereavement it seems to help if there is someone you can blame, however guiltless that person may be.

My eldest brother, Ron, was six years older than I was. Those years formed a chasm which I never successfully bridged. He was a lovable person. My mother adored him and was forever covering up the scrapes into which he constantly got himself. Ron enjoyed considerable success with the opposite sex and when he was tragically killed in the early part of the war, he was mourned by a number of young ladies who believed themselves his 'one and only love'. I wish I had known him better.

I was the youngest of the family. Next came Sylvia, a year older than myself, and then Geoffrey. My sister and I enjoyed a love-hate relationship. We fought like cat and dog — and she always won. Sylvia became a nurse and then married a farmer from Kenya. She now lives, with her four children, just outside Salisbury, Rhodesia.

Of all the family, I was closest to my brother Geoffrey. We were both psychic from earliest childhood. This formed a bond between us. Our world was populated by 'shadow people' who seemed invisible to the rest of the family. One aspect of this 'sense' which Geoffrey did not share with me was the ability to see coloured haloes of light surrounding people.

Psychic gifts are not easily carried. To a young child they represent an almost insupportable burden. It takes years before one learns how to construct a barrier of protection. If it were only a matter of seeing 'spirits', it might be straight-forward enough. Certainly some of the 'shadow people' seemed to be just that. But this was a rare phenomenon. The vast majority of these psychic impressions had a dreamlike quality. It was as if one were psychometrising time and reading its associations. For many years I could not enter a museum without becoming physically ill from the violent

27

assault the myriad impressions made upon me.

In retrospect, I would put up with all the misery this caused me over the years, just to preserve my gift for seeing the aura. I have devoted a great deal of time to research in this field and have gained much from it. One day, scientific analysis of the atmosphere of energy which surrounds every living creature may represent one of the most accurate methods of diagnosis available to man.

It may be possible, in this manner, to analyse the problems of the emotionally disturbed, both accurately and quickly, without years of analysis on a psychiatrist's couch. We may be able to trace the onset of disease before it becomes organically diagnosable.

Father was a director of a company manufacturing and marketing neon signs. As he prospered, so we moved from a three- to a four-bedroomed house and then, later, to a seven-bedroomed house, set in pleasant gardens, backing onto a golf course.

In the 1914-18 war my father added two years to his age and joined the Gordon Highlanders. It was his pride in this Regiment that inspired my Christian name. At sixteen he was fighting in Belgium, where he was wounded at the battle of Mons. He had very little formal education, leaving school at fourteen; but his handwriting, even to this day, is a perfect copperplate. He is a fighter, and this made him seem a tough father at times. But he provided us with a better home than he had ever known and it must have been difficult for him after my mother died to cope with four growing children.

With the exception, perhaps, of Geoffrey, we were not the easiest of children. If we felt strongly about anything we would dig our heels in and even father's firmly applied hand would not shift us.

Ron, Sylvia and I took after my father in appearance. We inherited his overlarge Roman nose and heavy build. Geoffrey was like my mother; having her delicate features and brown eyes. He was smaller than the rest of us and compensated for this with a truly fiery temper. When we fought I used to let him beat me because he so much minded losing. On one such occasion I put my tongue out at him. It required four stitches to sew it together again.

At Margate there were 'ghosts', but Geoffrey and I were able to share them. In any case, it was haunted by generations of happy boys. Young people do not mind discipline, what they cannot stand is stupid and cruel authoritarianism. The corridors of Margate echoed with the atmosphere of its previous occupants. The associations made one feel part of a well-ordered procession. I did not mind its ghosts.

Berkhamsted had 'ghosts' of a quite different character. One could feel the centuries of discipline through fear. It was haunted by its own past and from it derived its atmosphere. There was something about the place which was oppressive. The gargoyles in the 'Old Hall', which was my common room, had pulled hideous faces at each successive generation of boys for more than four hundred years. I wonder if they have now been exorcised by a more liberal regime.

I left Berkhamsted and worked for a short time in the offices of a firm of quantity surveyors until I was old enough to join the R.A.F.

The period I spent in the Air Force was neither particularly formative nor damaging. I learnt how to drink, smoke, swear and drive. At Berkhamsted we had been taught that the only people worth knowing were those who had been to a Public School. In the R.A.F. I learnt that 'good rock' is often to be found in the roughest quarries. Most of the Grammar School boys I met had had a better education than my Public School had been able to provide.

It was an interlude during a troubled time: neither more nor less. If memorable for nothing else, it was rich in companionship. I was discharged suffering from damage to the optic nerves. In my haste to obtain a quick 'discharge I refused further medical attention and thus forfeited my chances of a reasonable pension. What I obtained was a meagre pittance. I was blind for the best part of twelve months. Because I wanted my independence, I was prepared to put up with a degree of physical discomfort. My lodgings in Whitechapel were the cheapest to be found, and this left me less than three shillings a day on which to live. Like an animal creeping away to lick its wounds, I broke all contact with my family and friends.

This was a fallow period. Money was a desperate problem. I was far too proud to ask my father's help and my eyes prevented me from finding a job. What I did discover was the camaraderie of poverty.

Acquaintances at my lodgings would help me find my way to Billingsgate Fish Market where I would stand at the bottom of the steep hills waiting for the traditional cry of the porters:

"Up the Hill!"

Three or four of us would scramble for the back of a barrow laden with boxes of fish and shove with all our might, our feet scrabbling for purchase on the cobbles. Panting and gasping, at the top we would receive a threepenny piece for our pains. On a good morning you could make five shillings worth of scaly coins.

Quite the most important occurrence during this time was my introduction to a Buddhist monk from Ceylon named Nerada Thera. He became my first meditation teacher. When he returned to his own country he obtained for me an introduction to a Tibetan Zen Master under whom I was able to continue my studies.

My eyes gradually strengthened until misty forms resolved themselves into clear images. The joy of being able to read again was like nothing I have experienced before or since. I enrolled at London University to study Psychology and Sociology. For this I was given a very small grant which, in practice, proved insufficient to purchase even the books I would require.

When, at the age of fifteen, I had decided that I loved animals too much to become a vet, I had formulated a new ambition. I wanted to be a writer — not a journalist, a real writer: an author — no less. The subjects I had chosen seemed those most likely to create the 'great modern novel'. To what ridiculous conceits our youthful aspirations trick us!

It was still poverty: but with a difference. Student poverty may be squalid, but it bears no stigma of shame. It was terrific fun. I moved to Bloomsbury and shared digs with seven other young people, three of whom were students, two artists, a sculptor and a communist bricklayer from Dublin.

We organised ourselves on the basis of 'one eat, all eat'. Since the communist was the only one with a regular income we allowed him to organise a commune to his own immense satisfaction. He was paid on Thursdays and the money usually lasted until Monday morning. This meant we had to put up with a political lecture at three meals; but it sounded fairly reasonable on a full stomach.

I hunted for casual nightwork to support myself. The experience was tremendous. I queued with tramps to wash up at Lyons Corner House, waited table in restaurants, lifted crates of milk bottles at a large dairy and pulled pints of beer in any pub that would take me on.

Vacations brought the opportunity to save. Ideally the work I sought should provide me with my keep at the same time. Among the many varied jobs I tried were pea-picking while living with a Romany family in a horse-drawn caravan; boxing exhibition bouts in a fairground booth and doubling this up with collecting passengers' money on the chair-o-planes; working a pneumatic drill in Holborn, Kingsway; selling Sunday newspapers; distributing soapflakes from door to door; addressing envelopes; and once, and once only, walking up and down Oxford Street wearing a sandwich

31

board advertising an Indian palmist.

When my studies were concluded I felt ready to launch myself as an author. During the last year I had actually managed to save a little money. I rented a small cottage in North Devon for a month, and invested my savings in a typewriter – an evil-tempered machine which continually jammed and when freed shot its carriage onto the floor.

Day after day I sat in front of that typewriter staring at a blank piece of paper. It was hopeless. Every now and again I would struggle to compose two or three paragraphs and then, throughly elated with my own virtuosity, strut off to the local pub and quaff cider. In the morning I would read my efforts of the previous day and recognise it for what it was – pretentious and empty. Back to the impassive white face of another sheet of my dwindling paper supply.

I returned to London broke and discouraged. There was nothing else for it. I would have to become a journalist. But only as a temporary expedient, of course. To my intense surprise, Fleet Street did not welcome me with open arms. On the contrary, the few people who consented to give me an interview did their utmost to discourage me from adding yet another aspirant to the ranks of an already overcrowded profession.

For a time I attempted to free-lance. It was soul destroying. I could have papered the walls of my room with rejection slips. I lived, as I had done as a student, a hand to mouth existence, finding casual work by night so that I might write by day.

I was a slow learner, but at least I did learn. By tailoring my articles to the material which publications seemed to use, I started earning a few small cheques. I tried my hand at writing for the 'pulp' fiction market; (at that time the book market was flooded with cheap paper back fiction); and this led to my finding full-time work with a small publishing company. For the first time since leaving the Air Force I was able to eat regularly.

Chapter IV

Throughout all this time there had been an ebb and flow in my psychic life. At Berkhamsted and in the R.A.F. it had had to be pushed as far below the surface as possible, to enable me to survive. During my period of blindness it was more concentrated, to the point of becoming a source of nervous stress. My study of meditation had helped me to obtain some measure of control, but this was a long hard road.

My brother Geoffrey's early death at the age of twenty-four had affected me profoundly. I felt that he wished to contact me; but the prospect was, somehow, awesome. I had seen his body, a swollen lifeless shell, in the undertaker's chapel. My sister-in-law had asked me to make certain that the ring she had given him on their wedding day still remained on his fingers. But I had drawn back from touching his body. The assurances I later gave her were falsehoods of kindness. Since that time I had feared that I might one day see that corpse resurrected, accusing me of my guilt. And yet if my brother really wanted to communicate with me, had I the right to close the door from my side? It was a problem which troubled me.

I had made one attempt to pierce the veil. A woman I met through my meditation classes had fringe contact with the Spiritualist Movement. She invited me to attend a seance with a medium who was reputed to be able to produce physical phenomena — complete ectoplasmic figures which were able to speak with their own voices, just as in life.

This medium had twice been prosecuted for fraud under the old Witchcraft Act (now replaced by the Fraudulent Mediums Act which effectively gives Spiritualism official recognition as a religion). It was said that, although at times she had resorted to fraud for material gain, she had, in fact, genuine psychic powers.

The meeting was held in a house in South-West London. About twenty people were present who had paid one pound each for admittance. The medium was dressed in bulky black clothes and was seated behind a curtain which was stretched across one corner of the room, forming what we were told was a 'cabinet' in which the psychic power might be collected. She was very fat, had a broad Scots accent and looked rather flushed.

We sat in a rough circle, holding hands. The room was pitch dark, but a small red light had been fixed above the cabinet to illuminate the materialisations if they emerged.

A rather intense lady warned us that we might only touch the figures if we were first given permission by the 'guide', and that the production of sudden white light, such as a torch, would endanger the medium's life. Strategically placed in front of the 'cabinet' was a battery of cameras. These were to be manipulated by a gentleman named Leon Isaacs, who apparently had a considerable reputation for seance-room photography. We were assured that he had agreed not to take any pictures without the 'guide's' permission.

The equipment required for the seance was comparatively simple, two megaphones with a band of luminous paint around the broadest end (called trumpets), a tambourine similarly decorated and a tin whistle.

A short prayer was offered up to the 'Great Spirit' and then we were off. In order to generate the necessary psychic power we must sing. We started sedately with two or three hymns. One lady, with an extraordinarily shrill voice, was rather good at these.

"Speerieet Divaine," she incanted.

"Spirit Divine attend our prayer," we dutifully followed.

When she paused for breath, a man with a somewhat fruity voice took over with 'Bless 'em All' and 'She'll Be Coming

34

Round The Mountains When She Comes'. It sounded like closing time in a cockney pub on a Saturday night. From behind the curtain could be heard stertorous sounds coming from the medium. I wondered what would happen if she fell asleep. Would we have to keep up our caterwauling all night?

We were silenced by a paroxysm of coughing. The medium cleared her throat and we were addressed in deep affected tones. It did not sound like her voice; but then it did not sound like a man's voice either. It was a parody of a Music Hall comedienne imitating an Oxford accent. So that we might better understand the phenomena we were about to witness, we were to be given a scientific dissertation on the processes involved.

Another bout of coughing: more throat clearing and a new voice took over. This time pedantic and high pitched, its accent a mixture of Glasgow and fractured English. It went on and on and on. We heard about nuclear crucibles of the solar plexus: vibrations of the soul and cosmic harmonics. It was like no science I had ever heard before. Holding one's attention on the voice became a physical pain. There was a rustling as we shifted our bottoms on the hard wooden chairs. The darkness was pregnant with the unspoken thoughts: "Get on with it. This isn't what we've come here for. Let's have the ectoplasm."

The 'scientist' at last made his exit to a volley of relieved "God bless you's" and his place was taken by a travesty of a precocious child. The power was dropping — hardly surprising after twenty minutes of the 'scientist' — we must sing louder, quicker. What was the matter? Weren't we happy to be there?

"Yes!" we chorused, like kids at a pantomime. And we were off again with 'She'll Be Coming Round the Mountains'.

The luminous bands on the trumpets started to shiver and bob.

"Louder!" screamed the precocious child. "Sing louder!"

"She'll be wearing khaki bloomers when she comes . . ." roared fruity voice.

". . . khaki bloomers when she comes!" shrieked shrill voice.

"When she comes! When she comes!" we all bellowed in unison.

The trumpets rose, hovered for a moment and then moved slowly round the circle a foot or so above our heads. Their pace quickened until they were weaving around us in a pyrotechnic ballet of luminous paint.

"Louder!" cried the child.

Our efforts to comply reached the point of frenzy. The trumpets were streaks of green-grey light. One of them crashed against the wall and fell like a dead bird to the floor. Before we had time to mourn its passing the tambourine floated up to a height of about three feet and began to beat time to our singing in a most jolly manner. The whistle added its shrill tones in single breathless trills.

". . . pink pyjamas when she comes!" croaked fruity voice, hoarse with his exertions.

"Bash!" went the tambourine.

"Whee!" went the whistle.

"When she comes! When she comes!" we chorused together.

There was a loud thumping on one of the walls.

"God bless you, friend. Is that mother?" a woman's voice enquired reverently.

"I'm afraid it's the neighbours, love," said the woman who had given the introductory speech.

"Do you think we could sing a bit quieter now?" she asked the beastly child in hesitant tones.

"There's enough power for the moment; but you'll have to sing again soon," it threatened.

The surviving trumpet slowed down and moved round the circle as if seeking someone.

36

"Are you looking for me, dear?"

"Is it me?"

"God bless you, friend," the sitters encouraged.

It stopped.

"There, I knew it was for me," a voice said triumphantly. It was the woman who had greeted the thumps. "Is that you, Mum?"

A husky voice emitted from the trumpet:

"No."

"Tom? I knew it would be you, Tom."

"No."

"Alf? It must be Alf."

"I am Florence," whispered the trumpet. "Called Flo," it added in case of further mistaken identity.

There was a long, awkward pause.

"I'm afraid I don't know anyone of that name," she admitted regretfully.

"I do," said a man's voice eagerly from the other side of the circle. The trumpet streaked across to him gratefully.

"I knew it wasn't for me," said the woman in a tiny little voice.

For about half an hour the trumpet continued to give its husky messages of comfort. Gradually a pattern emerged. The cockneys had too cockney accents; Irishmen came straight from the stage of Collins' Music Hall; the Scots were too Glaswegian; the gasping, choking newly dead; and the Chinese guides who were "velly pleased to gleet us".

It had its own exaggerated and distinctive language, like the mime of a Punch and Judy show. Once the trumpet came to me. I acknowledged Mum and accepted her love. She was very happy in the spirit world. I was glad. If the rich aroma of whiskey coming from the trumpet was anything to go by she had good reason so to be.

After a further round of communal singing which tailed off in disarray in the face of furious thumping which

37

threatened to dislodge the plaster, we were ready for the 'ectoplasmic materialisations'.

The breathing behind the curtains reached proportions which were positively alarming.

"Perhaps if we sang . . . ," someone said tentatively.

No-one displayed enthusiasm. Next time the thumper might be through the wall and he sounded both big and very annoyed.

"I think it's the camera," suggested another voice. "They don't like cameras," it said authoritatively.

"Is it the cameras?" the organiser enquired of the cabinet. There was a noise somewhere between a snort and a grunt.

"There, I thought it was," said the voice who had suggested the idea. "These researchers don't mind what they do to her, poor soul. And when they've murdered her, will they be happy to let her rest? Not they!"

Mr. Isaacs protested his innocence of any such intent.

"Now!" called the horrible child from behind the curtain.

The dim red light revealed a white draped figure with long blond hair.

"Mother!"

"Dad!" greeted two voices simultaneously.

"Shall I take a picture?" pleaded Leon Isaacs.

The figure faded back into the cabinet. After further delays, we were treated to three more emergences, one brunette, one blonde and one in the head-dress of a North American Indian chief. All were claimed by several members of the circle, the Indian having particular success, with almost unanimous recognition.

After a mercifully short return visit from the 'scientist' the proceedings were brought to a close with a further prayer.

We chatted among ourselves as we waited for the medium to surface from the depths of her trance.

"I'm certain the first one was Mother," said the woman who had been unable to place Florence. "I recognised her features distinctly."

"I never got a picture after all that," said the poor photographer in a hurt voice.

"Isn't it exciting?" said the woman sitting beside me. "Just like Pentecost."

"I'll nip out and put the kettle on just as soon as she's back with us," said the organiser.

I suddenly realised that my bottom had gone quite dead on the hard wooden seat. I looked at my watch. We had been sitting there for over two hours.

I do not know what I had expected. Certainly nothing like that. As far as I was concerned the veil had not been rent — for that matter, it had not sustained so much as the smallest tear.

If anyone had told me that night that I would one day speak for the Spiritualist cause from the platform of the Royal Albert Hall to an audience of five thousand, I would have told them they were mad.

Chapter V

Life should have been happy. I had a good job in a publishing house. There was every opportunity for succeeding with my writing. My financial situation had improved. I had a pleasant flat. My health was good. I was in my mid-twenties and at last fate seemed to be smiling upon me.

But I was still deeply troubled about my brother Geoffrey. I· dreamt about him repeatedly. The faint odour of death, which I had noticed in the undertaker's chapel when I went to see his body, seemed to permeate my flat. If I opened the windows wide it would clear for a few minutes; but as soon as they were closed it would return again. I felt that he wanted to contact me, but I was still afraid.

I discovered a small Spiritualist church in the Kings Cross area of London. With two friends, I attended a few meetings. The story of how this settled my fears about my brother and led to the discovery of my healing gift, has been fully told in my previous book *An Outline of Spiritual Healing.*

The meetings at this church were sometimes interesting, although on occasion they were pretty bad. It was, in a funny sort of way, convincing that the mediums were so variable. When they were off form, it showed the clear difference between their gift and plain guesswork. In general, they were rather unintelligent and, I would have thought, incapable of sustained deception.

Unlike the lady in the seance I have described, these mediums did not claim to produce ectoplasm, relying upon mental powers such as clairvoyance for their messages.

The one exception was a one-legged medium who gave transfiguration seances. In theory, ectoplasm formed over his face and was then moulded like a mask to resemble the features of the spirit communicating.

In practice, his technique was more mundane. He would sit on an upright wooden chair. In front of him was a card table with a converted car headlamp on it, fitted with a dim red bulb. With the aid of books to achieve the desired tilt, the lamp was directed to shine upwards onto his face. He would tuck a piece of black material into his collar to hide his shirt and then say a short prayer.

The niceties having been duly regarded, he would take out a handkerchief in which he would wrap his upper and lower dentures. The extra elasticity this gave his features, together with the shadows cast by the red lamp, enabled him to produce some startling 'transfigurations'.

Once again, a most interesting feature of these meetings was the total lack of any critical standards displayed by the majority of those attending. It seemed to worry them not at all that a face presented as Alice might be lovingly accepted as Charlie. They would swallow sex change or alter ego without question.

The medium had a distinct Midlands accent which was shared by all spirits communicating through his 'powers'. Chang, his Chinese guide, was a delightful creation, combining the best of Mr. Wu's Chinese laundry with the broad speech of the Potteries.

On one occasion I presumed to question the authenticity of a 'face' claiming to be my paternal grandmother — at that time very much with us on earth. The other people present tutted and muttered at my firm denial.

"Poor old lady," someone said. "Fancy turning away your own Grannie."

There was an attempt to tranform her into my maternal grandmother, which I again resisted, and then into Uncle Fred.

Finally, Chang came to the rescue.

"Since you do not accept spirits you no geteee message,"

41

he said firmly. To the room at large he announced: "Old lady would have tell him he would have won football pools. Now he not get plize."

"And a good thing too!" said a woman at the back.

I decided to have my own back on Chang. He had been having everything his own way for too long.

The next time a 'transfiguration' seance was advertised, I took along an acquaintance who managed a Chinese restaurant. I made certain we had seats slap bang in the middle of the front row.

In walked the medium, nodding and smiling to his friends in the audience. He noticed us and for a moment his smile froze. As he tucked in the black cloth, he eyed us carefully. I had a feeling that Chang might be urgently called away on higher matters.

But no. Devotions and dentures having been despatched, there was Chang, as large as life after death, beaming and bowing as he 'gleeted' us in broad Midland pidgin. My Oriental friend stood up, placed his two hands together, bowed and launched into a rattle of what appeared to be Chinese compliments.

There was a shocked silence. But Chang was a quick thinker.

"My fliend and fellow countlyman," he said. "Your sentiments do you gleat cledit. We accept them and bless you for their wisdom. But let us lemember we are the guests of these fine people. It would be bad manners to speak in a language they cannot understand."

There was a loud sigh of relief from the audience. Chang gave me a little nod as if to say: "Get round that one!"

As we left the building I turned to my friend.

"By the way, what was it you said to him with all that bowing and scraping?"

His eyes twinkled.

"Twenty-four portions of sweet and sour dog droppings,

42

stirred up in a bucket of pig food and tipped over your esteemed head."

I put my hands together and bowed my appreciation.

The public meetings were becoming less and less interesting as I became accustomed to their stereotyped format. I became more selective. I realised that not everyone who was interested in Spiritualism was a gullible fool.

There was, for instance, an extraordinary old man named Mr. Gray. He claimed to be ninety-seven years old. His skin was fresh pink and white and his eyes a penetrating blue. He was an astrologer and a 'colour-healer'.

Astrology has always seemed to me a pseudo-science based on postulates which are fundamentally inaccurate. Its practitioners insist that it is a precise science; but I am sure that good astrologers are psychics who subconsciously use their charts and almanacs as a focal point on which to concentrate their gift — in much the same way that a clairvoyant uses a crystal ball. One thing I would hesitate to denigrate is the remarkable accuracy displayed by some astrologers.

Mr. Gray was not a professional in the monetary sense of the word. He would occasionally accept a small gift, but this was not expected and in no way affected the availability of his services.

He was always on duty. In the basement of the converted shop which was the Kings Cross Spiritualist Church, there was a room referred to as the canteen. Tea was served in jam jars and sandwiches and cakes were supplied by loyal supporters. This was the old man's favourite hunting ground.

He would sit there, sipping his jar of tea and examining any new faces with quick, birdlike movements of his head. Sometimes he would decide the moment was propitious. It was only when he went to stand up that you realised he was a very old man. He would rise piece by piece: knees, hips, back and front: when he was finally upright, his carriage was as erect as any guardsman.

Mr. Gray had a disarming old world courtesy. He would first give a stiff little bow and then produce a yellowing visiting card from his top pocket. When he was satisfied that you had been given time to digest its contents, he would restore it to his pocket and fold himself into a chair beside you.

The first time this happened to me, I was too absorbed in thought to observe his approach. There was a polite little cough and I became aware of the card held under my nose. I went to take it, but he kept his finger and thumb firmly gripping the corner. It was too precious to be risked out of his direct control. The card informed me that its owner was a Master Metaphysician.

Safely installed in a chair, he studied me for a full two minutes without speaking. The experience was slightly unnerving.

"Aries, I think?" he said.

"I beg your pardon?"

"You were born under the sign of Aries, I think? Early in the sign, I would say."

"April 1st," I replied.

"Just so. That explains a great deal." He positively beamed with satisfaction.

There followed a brief character analysis, which, if a little uncomplimentary, was surprisingly accurate. I thanked him and waited to see what would follow, expecting a list of his charges and an address at which he would be prepared to give me a longer sitting. I was doing him an injustice. He just prattled on about his psychic experiences and finally excused himself and creaked back to the vertical.

After this, we often had a chat. I discovered that when the church was closed he would hold court at a nearby Lyons teashop. On several occasions I visited him there, to find him surrounded by a small coterie of devotees.

His versatility seemed unbounded. He gave astrological

advice, stared into palms, read tarot cards and gave psycho-metrical readings by holding small articles such as keys or letters. On one occasion he even produced a crystal ball which he placed on a piece of black cloth, and solemnly peered into the future amid the litter of baked beans and toasted teacakes.

I enjoyed talking to Mr. Gray. His credulity was almost childlike and yet, despite this, he was a well-educated man. I often wondered about his background. He was widely travelled and his experiences seemed boundless. At different times I settled on clergyman, schoolmaster, solicitor and minor diplomat. But he was reluctant to reveal anything which might give a clue to his circumstances.

Certainly, he was very poor. He always wore the same navy blue suit — ill pressed, shining like glass, but impeccably clean. His shoes shone brightly, but on the occasions when he crossed his creaky legs, he revealed their paper thin soles with holes through to his socks. The one incongruity with his neat appearance was his pockets which bulged as if carrying his entire worldly estate. This, in fact, I believed to be the case, until one day he offered to treat me by 'colour healing'.

I had strained my back playing rugby and moved with obvious discomfort. He saw me across the canteen and made his way over to join me. I did not regard his offer very seriously, but accepted it from curiosity as much as anything.

In no time, he had cleared two tables on which I was to be stretched full length. From his pockets he started to draw lengths of coloured muslin, muttering as he went:

"Red for pain. Yes, definitely red. I dye all these myself, you know, dear chap. Have you right in no time, but we must get the colours right, you see. A little green to relax the muscles, and yellow for the nerves. Marvellous colour for the nerves, yellow."

And so it went on until he resembled Salome's dresser preparing her for her celebrated dance. I realised why his pockets looked so bulky.

At his instruction, I hefted myself up onto the improvised couch and tried to peer over my shoulder to watch what he was doing. First I was draped with the red muslin.

"Now for the pain," said Mr. Gray.

He bent over me and puffed and blew with all his might. When he was satisfied, he removed the cloth, waved back a small group of admirers who had clustered round, and shook the cloth with all his might. Thus, we were told, he was shaking off the bad vibrations.

"Now for the tight muscles," he said.

The blowing reached gale force. His usually pink face was turning purple. By the time he reached the yellow I was seriously alarmed. He was staggering, gasping and clutching his chest. I leapt off the table and helped him to a chair, placing a jar of tea in his shaking hands. He was so breathless it took minutes before he could even sip it.

"Don't worry. It's nothing, my dear young friend. I've just taken on your conditions. I'll clear it in no time." He drew his precious lengths of cloth about him and shrank into them for comfort.

This was terrible. If I had known that the poor old man was going to finish up with my back-ache, I would never have allowed him to try. So disturbed was I, that it was not until I was getting ready for bed, several hours later, that I realised that I had no trace of pain in my back.

I wish it were possible to complete the story of Mr. Gray. I stopped going to the church for a couple of months and when I returned he was not there. I enquired for him, but no-one knew where he lived or anything about him. He was not at his usual table in the teashop and the manageress said he had not been there for several weeks. I never saw him again. That is the way of big cities. If you live in them it has to be accepted. He was a good man with a fine simplicity of soul. I learned much from him without realising the degree to which I was absorbing his influence.

At this time my thinking with regard to Spiritualism was somewhat ambivalent. I had been born a 'sensitive' and therefore did not require proof of the existence of psychic abilities in others. But many Spiritualists were a bit hard to stomach. Madame Bodini, for example.

Madame Bodini was the old lady who dispensed tea in the canteen. She was a White Russian and claimed distant ancestry with the ill-fated Czar. Madame fancied herself no end of a medium. The only problem was that no-one would willingly sit with her — certainly not twice, anyway. Like all newcomers to the church, I was trapped before I knew what I was letting myself in for.

I had arranged to join a group of six people, which was to be taken by a young clairvoyant named Peter Shelton. In my opinion he was the most promising of the mental mediums I had sampled thus far. On my arrival I noticed that the canteen was emptier than usual. The medium, I was told, was ill. Madame Bodini, a celebrated medium of many years' standing, had consented to come out of retirement to fill the gap. I was suitably impressed.

Madame appeared to have prepared for the occasion. Gone were the overall and faded headscarf of her tea-pouring role. In their stead she had donned the most incredible assortment of finery. At one time she must have been a much more petite woman. The black and gold floor-length gown was stretched to breaking. Every breath tested its ancient cotton seams in a most alarming manner.

The predominant influence was Ancient Egyptian. Scarabs crawled hungrily all over her ample person. The little green beetles appeared everywhere: under her bosom, round the high neck of her gown, in the act of disappearing under her arms — they seemed to have established unchallenged possession of her person. If the stones which encrusted her fingers had been real, they would have been worth a king's ransom.

Her yellow-grey hair was piled high upon her head and topped by a hideous tiara. But most awesome of all was her face. Chalk white with layers of make-up, the mouth was a ghastly scarlet wound. She smiled at me and her face cracked into a crazing of little lines and began to crumble.

Madame beckoned to me to follow her. It was not until we were in the room set aside for the circle that the frightful truth dawned. The other sitters had backed out. Only two chairs had been arranged, closely facing each other. She bolted the door and switched on a blue light. What had appeared awful in normal light was rendered positively ghoulish by the blue bulb. She settled herself into her chair, opened her handbag and popped what I thought was a sweet into the scarlet gash.

"Now I speak to the spirits in their own tongue. Then they will come. Many of them," she promised. She waved her arms expansively and there was an alarming sound of tearing material.

Madame Bodini threw back her head. I could see the whites of her eyes. At tremendous speed she spouted what seemed gibberish. Her body rocked backwards and forwards at an ever quickening tempo. The seams of her gown strained and ripped. I sniffed suspiciously and nearly gagged. The 'sweet' had been a clove of garlic.

Madame subsided not a stitch too soon. Her 'jewelled' fingers darted into her handbag and recharged her mouth with another clove. She leant forward, placed her hand upon my knee and brought her face up to mine.

"Your father, he is in the world of spirits?"

Almost suffocating, I consigned my much-alive father to eternity. Anything for escape!

"Ah! He is here. And your sister?"

Without qualm I sacrificed poor Sylvia. In quick succession I lost my only surviving uncle, my paternal grandmother and two of my best friends. It was uncanny. She hit on those still living every time. I tried to pull my chair back, but she followed inexorably. We processed the small seance room accompanied by scraping chair legs and ripping seams.

At last I could bear no more. I pulled out my handkerchief and held it to my nose. There was no need to feign tears; they were streaming down my cheeks.

"Madame, I am overcome," I said truthfully — and fled.

After that momentous evening I never again entered the canteen without receiving a message of encouragement from my 'dear Papa'. Slowly, a picture of him emerged. He was a tall, thin, military gentleman, dressed in a blazer, flannel trousers and a Panama hat. Later were added brown and white shoes and a red carnation in his buttonhole. Subsequent additions, such as a monocle and a thin scar on his left cheek, gave him a definite air. I grew quite fond of the old chap.

I was persuaded to join a developing circle. These comprised small groups of people interested in bringing out whatever psychic faculties they might possess. I had, quite literally, reached the extent of my interest in Spiritualism as a religion: but I still wanted to resolve the problem which had originally brought me to the church.

I am not by nature a religious man. Formal services seem to me stilted and repetitious. I feel more sense of an Omnipotent Presence in a forest, in mountains, or under a star-filled sky than in places of religious worship. I find spoken prayer intensely embarrassing.

When I was a child, I am told, I was taken to church by my nanny, a devout Catholic. On the way home I asked:

"Why were those people singing?"

"They were singing to God, dear," she replied.

"Why?"

"Because it is Sunday," I was told.

"Do they sing to Him every Sunday?" I asked.

"Yes, dear," my nanny said, pleased at my interest. "Not only here, but in thousands of churches all over the world."

I considered this information.

"Poor God!" I said.

To this day, I still feel rather sorry for God on Sundays.

Spiritualist Sunday services are not dissimilar to those of other non-conformist religious groups. The hymns are set to well-known tunes and prayers are given spontaneously. There is a reading from the Bible or, occasionally, some other book which appeals to the person conducting the service. One feature which is unique is the demonstration of clairvoyance. A medium describes deceased friends and relatives to the congregation, sometimes conveying messages which she believes she hears clairaudiently or senses through mental impressions.

I remember one occasion when a rather nervous tyro-medium was attempting to give her first demonstration of public clairvoyance. She addressed a stout lady at the back of the room who was scowling ominously.

"I am seeing a little baby. They are showing me a newly born baby in the spirit world, with you," she declared hopefully.

"Nothing to do with me," said the woman.

"But I'm sure it must be," the medium pleaded.

"You haven't told me much about it," the woman argued. "You'll have to give me something more evidential than that."

"I've got it!" shouted the medium triumphantly. "It's a little boy. They are turning it round and showing it to me."

The only Spiritualist religious service I attended at this time was conducted by a stout cockney medium who ran a 'church' in her own home. We were being treated to an impassioned address on the sanctity of all life and God's love for the entire animal kingdom.

"We've got to luv' 'em all," we were told. " 'Cos 'e loves 'em just as 'e loves us. It don't matter wot they are or wot they do: yer got to luv' 'em."

A small black mongrel dog pushed its nose round the door, sniffed, and started its way up the narrow aisle between the chairs. It caught the medium's eye and she faltered slightly.

" 'Cos 'e's entrusted 'em to our luvvin' care. So we got to be good to 'em — 'aven't we?"

The small dog found a particularly interesting piece of carpet and sniffed carefully.

Somehow, the medium managed to keep one eye on the dog and fix the congregation with the other.

"For 'oosoever 'armeth one o' them little ones . . ." She stopped. The dog had opened wide its back legs and was relieving itself on the carpet.

Despite her girth, the medium was off the rostrum in seconds and had it by the scruff of the neck, shaking it vigorously as she conveyed it to the door and hurled it out.

"That filthy little beast does that in 'ere every time she gets in," she complained bitterly. One or two ladies tutted and clucked their sympathy.

The medium took a deep breath and recovered her equilibrium. She continued her address as she made her way back to the rostrum.

"Yerss, yer got to luv 'em, wotever they do, sweet little innercents, just as 'e does," she instructed us earnestly.

The developing circle in which I found myself was conducted by a man called Frank Berger. He was in his late fifties. By day he worked for the Railways as an electrician, and at night he took up his chosen vocation as a medium.

Frank, like nearly all the Spiritualists I have met, was utterly sincere and kind to a fault. He lived with his wife and two children in a basement in one of the dreary streets behind Kings Cross Station. He became a friend and suggested I join him in his weekly healing session.

I had quite inadvertently accrued a modest reputation as a healer. At one of the public clairvoyance demonstrations the medium had said that he thought I was a natural healer. As

51

the meeting dispersed, a man limped up to me and asked if I could do anything about his back, which he had injured at work.

Rather embarrassed, I sat him on a chair, rubbed his back a bit, and then gave it a push with the heel of my hand. He declared himself cured and did not hesitate to sing my praises. Quite quickly, I added to this a migraine sufferer and, of all people, Madame Bodini, who was convinced I had healed her arthritic knee.

Frank Berger did his healing by means of a complicated series of hand-passes. He believed that he had been taught these by his spirit guide. I subsequently discovered that they were very similar to those used by Franz Anton Mesmer (1733-1815).

It was essential, Frank believed, that the healer's breathing should be perfectly co-ordinated with these passes. Inhaling, the hands were drawn, fingers pointed, and thumb to thumb, over the sick part of the body: breath held, the hands were drawn clear of the patient in a clockwise direction, and then flicked outwards with sufficient vigour to 'splat' the fingers in the process. This, he believed, 'shook off the diseased ectoplasm'.

I was hopeless. I was breathing in when I should have been breathing out. My hands moved in the wrong direction: even worse, my fingers would not produce so much as the smallest 'splat'. Frank tried to be patient with me, but it was of no avail. When a small group decided to form a new circle and move to the home of one of the members, I reluctantly decided to join them.

At the first meeting they voted and to my astonishment unanimously elected me their leader. When they persuaded me to abide by their decision they were, without realising it, changing the whole course of my life.

Chapter VI

We held our weekly developing circle at Stoke Newington in North London, in the parlour of a dressmaker. There were twelve of us, mostly under thirty, and all very open-minded. We read books; tried psychic experiments; but always returned to the subject of healing.

I was still being asked to give healing to a variety of people. The sister of the dressmaker was taken ill and medically diagnosed as suffering from gall stones. After healing she passed them and an operation was averted. She wrote to a newspaper telling her story. As a result of her letter absolute strangers began to seek my services.

It was like a snowball. Everyone who felt better told their friends. I was asked to look at a young boy with a displaced hip. His father was the editor of a local newspaper — a fact unknown to me at the time. He was so thrilled with his son's recovery that he printed a front-page story. I was inundated with would-be patients.

I was very conscious of the responsibilities I was being asked to accept, and was at pains to ensure that those seeking my help were not doing so as an alternative to proper medical advice. After much heart searching, I left my job with the publishing house and enrolled at University to study anatomy and physiology. As there was no chance of a grant, I obtained part-time employment with an Indian brass importer.

By so reducing my material circumstances I could no longer afford to keep my flat. This was a dreadful wrench. I had been through so much unsettlement since leaving school that my need for domestic security was almost pathological.

I moved into the top room of a house rented by a member of the circle. The only running water was a tap on the landing below, and the lavatory was at the end of a concrete yard at the back of the house. To obtain a bath I had to visit the public municipal baths, a short bus ride away.

Automatically, I saw less and less of my old friends and acquaintances. Many of them were seriously concerned about my absorption with psychic matters and healing. It was difficult for them to understand why I should deliberately sacrifice all that I had worked so hard to achieve. I did not try to explain.

As far as I was concerned, there was no question of choice. I had a gift which, it appeared, could help others — even some who were incurable by more orthodox means. It was not something I had chosen: seemingly, it had selected me. If this was the case, I could not play at it as a dilettante: I had to be a professional. Such was my temperament. I had inherited my father's stubbornness, together with a measure of his dogged determination.

I needed somewhere to see my patients. The lady in whose house I was lodging offered me her coal cellar. When I inspected it my heart sank. It was below ground level and without windows. Damp was mouldering the brick walls and the plaster ceiling was sagging ominously.

Two members of the circle volunteered to help. They had some small experience of healing and wanted to work with me when the premises were ready. The whole job cost a little more than £10. We constructed a frame of wooden slats round the walls and over the ceiling and then nailed heavy duty oilcloth to cover the whole. This served the dual purpose of insulating the room from damp and providing a surface onto which we could paste wallpaper. A great discovery was the remains of an old chimney breast in one of the walls. We opened it up and built a large farm-kitchen type fireplace. From the moment we lit our first fire, the whole room took on a more cheerful aspect. We combed junk shops for chairs and pieces of furniture. In no time at all we were ready to open. We named it, somewhat grandiosely, 'The Sanctuary of Healing'. Alf, a Post Office engineer, and his young wife Sylvia, joined me as assistants. They had worked like Trojans preparing the cellar-sanctuary and had done a little healing at their local Spiritualist church. Alf was a character. Cockney through and through, his large round spectacles and blinking myopic eyes gave him something of the appearance of a benevolent owl. Sylvia, who was only seventeen, worked as a typist. She was a sweet girl.

Our first patient was a tortoise. It was brought by a little boy, who watched solemnly while his pet was healed.

Animals of all sorts respond wonderfully to healing. I have subsequently treated every kind of domestic pet and farm-yard animal, with considerable success. Among more unusual creatures a bear, an elephant and an otter stand out. I have never been bitten or scratched: this despite the fact that I make it a point of honour not to treat an animal in a muzzle or which has been anaesthetised.

We held our 'clinics' on Tuesday and Thursday evenings. About thirty patients attended each session. We charged no fees, but left a plate in the hall for anyone who wanted to leave a voluntary contribution. On a good night we collected about a pound. This just covered our light and heat. The telephone, a great luxury we had rather ambitiously had installed, we split with the bookmaker's runner who lived next door — unashamedly making a small profit from his endless calls about doubles and trebles.

My part-time job with the Indian brass importer ended abruptly. He had a son of about eighteen who strutted, roaring and swearing, among the women employed on polishing. I sat at an upturned tea chest, checking endless columns of figures. It was sweated labour and every week it grew more difficult to extract my hard-earned money.

One day the unpleasant son decided to vent his temper on me. He stood over me, beating me about the head and face with a rolled up newspaper. It was too much. I carried him over to the window, stuck him out up to the waist and jammed it tightly shut. With his trousers down to his ankles, I gave him the wopping he so richly deserved. The women screamed encouragement, but his shrieks were the loudest. I did not wait to collect the money owing to me. It would have been an anti-climax.

Part-time work is always harder come by than regular employment. Eventually, I found a job in a laundry. I was handling sacks and drums of chemicals. It was desperately hard. My hands broke out in a rash and the fumes gave me asthma. I had to leave.

My luck changed. I was employed by an old family business in the City of London, selling wholesale drapery. The two brothers who ran the firm were the fifth generation in unbroken line. They were kind to a fault.

I had told them of my other interests when applying for the job. Although I was only a part-time floor salesman — just about the lowest form of animal life in a drapery warehouse — they gave me an office of my own, so that I might have the chance to cope with my rapidly growing postbag while waiting for the customers to come in. I wish I could have justified their trust better. I am just not a salesman. As far as I was concerned, one blanket looked exactly like another.

Most of our customers had market stalls or small shops. They paid in cash for their goods and took them away with them. It did not take them long to discover they had a mug on their hands. They queued for my attention and brought their relatives with them. They purchased best quality goods at bargain prices. Patiently, the brothers called me in and tried to explain the difference between cotton and wool.

A warehouseman at this firm was the nephew of Harry Champion, the great music hall comedian, and looked just like him. He could go right through his uncle's act in superb imitation. Strangely, he was a most lugubrious man when not performing. He regarded me, possibly astutely, as quite unworthy of the firm's employ and never hesitated to report any mistakes of mine he might discover.

I was interviewed by a popular weekly magazine which featured my cellar-sanctuary in most patronising terms. I have never believed the cliché 'all publicity is good publicity', but, in this case, it brought a veritable avalanche of interest.

Unfortunately, I had innocently mentioned my part-time job. When I arrived at the warehouse on Monday, there was a queue waiting outside. All day long I healed the sick among bales of blankets and carpets.

Patient as ever, the brothers told me: "Don't worry, Turner. It's a five-day wonder. Cope as best you can. Everything will be back to normal next week."

They were too optimistic. A City newspaper picked up the story and gave it a middle-page spread the following Friday. By Monday the queue was longer than ever. It was ridiculous. I should have been paying the poor brothers. I had to do something to make it up to them.

I noticed a well-dressed man with a diamond tie-pin, watching me while I healed. I walked over to him.

"Can I help you, Sir?" I asked in my best salesman voice.

"That's very nice of you, son. Not disturbing you, am I?"

"Not at all, Sir. That's what I'm employed here for," I said in a business-like way.

"I had wondered," he said, drily. "I tell you what, you're new here, aren't you? Well, just to give you a start I'll let you handle my order."

He snapped his fingers and two brown-coated workmen were at his side. It was an immense order, over five hundred pounds worth of goods, all selected from the same heap, stacked nearest the door. He signed the order form and gave me his business card.

I filed the order with considerable pride. This at least

57

c

would make up a little for the kindness I had been shown.

The next morning one of the brothers was waiting for me when I arrived.

"There was a large pile of goods here, Turner. Did you see what happened to them?"

"I've sold them all, Sir," I said proudly. "The order is filed."

"To this person?" He was holding my customer's card.

"That's right, Sir."

He put his hands to his head and groaned.

"He's a knocker. He's got no shop, nothing! We'll never pin him down. Anyway, he's in the clear. We gave him credit: it's our own stupid fault. Didn't you look at the Knockers' List?"

There was a pink sheet pinned inside all the sales order books with a list of customers who did not pay their bills and from whom we had to have cash.

"You know, Turner, I've worked here since I left school. I've never known us sack anyone in all that time." His voice was sad and tired. "People have left of their own accord, of course, but they've always given us notice. Quite a record, that. I'd hate to see it broken."

At last there was something I could do and get it right.

"Sir," I blurted. "I've got to leave. Terribly sorry and all that."

"Oh, have you, Turner? I am sorry. If it will help you at all we won't hold you to working notice. If you pop up to the office in about ten minutes, we'll have a couple of weeks' money ready for you."

He turned on his heel to go and then called over his shoulder: "Er . . . please don't trouble to sell anything while you're waiting, Turner. In fact, don't do anything."

As I was leaving, the warehouseman sidled up to me. He looked smugly satisfied.

" 'Ere! Yer know that smutter yer flogged the knocker?

Well, that was all best quality put aside for —." He named our best customer. "Dead narked 'e was. Cancelled 'is order an' all." I felt terrible. They had deserved better of me.

The really big decisions in life have about them a certain inevitability. I had a sanctuary and plenty of people wanting me to treat them. I decided to devote my entire time to healing.

Now, the collection plate really mattered. During the day I saw patients at allotted intervals and in the evening held open clinics. We were so busy, I invited Bill and Doris — another husband and wife — to join the team.

Despite the volume of work, the plate seldom yielded more than one pound for the entire day's work. I began to learn a little about the strange psychology of generosity. Some people left nothing and the majority sixpence. Occasionally, somebody would leave as much as ten shillings. The poor people tended to be more generous than those who were obviously quite well off. There was a steady trickle of farthings and foreign coins: too many to have been slipped into the collection by accident.

My sanctuary was in one of London's poorest districts. The majority of my patients lived nearby, but some travelled long distances to see me. It was not uncommon for a Rolls Royce to be parked outside my door, a fact which delighted the local children. While I was treating the owner, the poor chauffeur would try to fight off a horde of squealing kids. They would unscrew the mascot, scramble over the bonnet and even pinch the tool kit, if given half a chance.

The attitude of some of these wealthy patients was quite extraordinary. They would thank me profusely and ask my fees.

"I don't charge a set fee. There's a collection plate on the hall table. You may leave what you like."

"I say! That's wonderful. You're doing fine work. Of course I'd like to support it. Tell you what. I'll leave a really big donation at the end of my treatment."

They never did. One millionaire who was suffering from a malignant blood disease promised to donate a fitted carpet for the sanctuary when he was healed. After about five treatments his hospital tests were clear. The specialist told him that his case must have been one of mistaken diagnosis. He telephoned excitedly and told me the news.

"Now, about that carpet. Can you be at home tomorrow afternoon? I'll bring the patterns round personally."

Of course he never showed up. Years later I walked into a restaurant and he was seated at the table opposite mine. Although he was only half way through the meat course, he grabbed his coat and fled.

The most blatant case of this kind I can remember was a man who was wheeled in to see me in a bath chair. He'd arrived in a chauffeur-driven Rolls Royce and was accompanied by a manservant.

"I have been like this for two years," he told me, "and I've spent a fortune trying to find a cure. I've been the length of Harley Street, to clinics in Switzerland; even Lourdes. In fact, everywhere. If you can cure me, you can name your own fee."

I gave him the same answer I gave everyone at that time.

"There's a collection plate in the hall. Leave what you like. In any case, I can't promise to heal you."

I gently ran my fingers down his spine. They reacted strongly to a spot near the base in the area of the fifth lumbar vertebra. I concentrated for a moment and then pressed it gently with my hand. There was a loud crack.

"Try to stand," I told him. "Your legs may feel weak from lack of use."

He stood up, wobbled and then took two or three paces.

"Good God! I haven't done that for two years." As he gathered confidence, he strode up and down, sat, stood up again, touched his toes and lifted his knees up and down like

60

a guardsman marking time.

"It's a miracle," he told me. "I'll never forget what you've done for me." He left pushing his own wheel-chair.

My curiosity got the better of me and I followed him up to the hall to see what he would leave. When he reached the plate he took out his wallet, hesitated, and put it away again. Reaching into his trousers pocket he extracted a handful of small change. He carefully placed a two shilling piece in the empty plate and opened the front door. He hesitated for a moment, and then returned to the plate, removed the florin and, having replaced it with a threepenny piece, hurried out of the front door.

I had resolved, when I had decided to try to develop such gifts as I might possess as a healer, not to read other people's ideas on the subject until such time as my own methods had found a natural pattern. After every healing session, I would analyse all that I had done and try to be clear how much was unnecessary embellishment on my part. In this way I managed to keep my work essentially simple.

Before attempting to heal the patient, I would stand behind his chair, resting the palms of my hands lightly on his shoulders. I would clear my mind and try to 'sense' the person I was about to treat.

After a few moments, I became aware of his feelings. If he were in pain, I would sense its echo in my own body. With practice the acuteness of my sensitivity made it possible for me to rely on my feelings during these moments of attunement.

I would then let my hands move lightly over the patient's body. As long as I could still my conscious mind they would be drawn to the exact spot where the treatment was needed. My slowly expanding knowledge of anatomy and physiology was a great help. I would envisage healthy organs in place of those that were diseased. If there was an adjustment of the bones to be made, it was essential that I avoided thinking

61

about what my hands were doing — for that matter even looking at them. Healing had to be a spontaneous rather than an intellectual matter.

Healing involved the transmission of energy — I was sure of that. I could feel this flowing through me. If my attunement had been made too casually, or if I became too personally involved in the healing, it would be my own energy which was drawn upon. But if the attunement was good and my mind clear, I could feel the healing power flowing through me from some apparently inexhaustible source. On such occasions I could heal for hours without tiring.

The reactions of the neighbours to my sanctuary were mixed. On the whole they were pretty tolerant, but if I went into the little corner shop, all conversation ceased instantly. As I left I would hear it resumed in hushed tones. A small minority were downright hostile. One night I was wakened by a drunken voice under my window.

" 'Ere, you up there! You that's supposed to be an 'ealer. If you're an 'ealer come down 'ere an' put me in a trance!"

I was just about to put my head out of the window and deliver myself of one or two unspiritual epithets, when a half brick smashed the glass to smithereens.

I gave this incident quite a lot of thought. Obviously, the man had not the faintest idea what I was doing. His attack had been triggered by ignorance. It was not fair to blame him for believing that I was indulging in some sort of outlandish ritual. No-one had explained differently to him. Healing was far from having the wide acceptance it enjoys today. The following morning I was in the corner shop almost as soon as it was open.

"Good morning. I hear you had a spot of bother last night. I am sorry." The lady who ran the shop always knew everything that had happened in the street.

"Thank you. That's what I've come in to talk to you about."

She froze. "Can't help you, I'm afraid. I haven't the slightest idea who did it."

"That isn't what I was going to ask you. I want to know exactly what the people round here have been saying about me. I don't want any names and I won't mind what you say."

"Nothing nasty, I'm sure. Milly Watson is thrilled with what you've done for her back . . ." She tailed off.

"But?"

"Well, some o' them don't think it's right. Playing with fire, it is. Nothing personal, you understand, but some people don't hold with magic and such like. We've never had anything like it in this street before."

I explained to her what I planned to do. I would take the local Co-operative Hall and invite everyone living in the street to attend a public healing session. They would have free admission, and afterwards I would answer their questions. Would she help me by trying to encourage them to come along? She agreed somewhat reluctantly.

When I stopped to think about the idea in cold blood it terrified me. I knew that a healer named Harry Edwards conducted public healing sessions, but I had never been to such a meeting, let alone organised one and done the healing. What would happen if no-one showed any sign of improvement? Worse, what if nobody turned up?

Once again, without knowing it, my life had reached another turning point.

Chapter VII

At this time my experience of public speaking was very limited. I had been invited to speak at a morning service in the Balham Spiritualist Church. I was so nervous then that my shaking was visible from the back of the hall. Once as a student I had accepted a dare to stand up at Speakers' Corner in Hyde Park — I managed to last thirty minutes, but I had been petrified despite the vocal support of my friends.

The meeting at the Co-operative Hall was a relatively small affair. It was attended by about forty people — twenty or so friends and patients and the remainder curious to see what it was all about.

As I treated about ten people, I explained in conversational tones what I was doing. It was, I suppose, a minor success. Several of those receiving healing showed immediate improvement. Two reporters attended and both wrote favourable accounts. One appeared in a Spiritualist newspaper and the other in the local press.

Whether this reached the small antagonistic element living near the sanctuary, it was hard to tell: at least there were no more bricks thrown at my window.

A direct outcome was that the press reports attracted the attention of George Cregeen. George worked for the *Evening Argus* in Brighton and edited a monthly horoscope magazine in his spare time. He was a healer of considerable ability and experience. He wrote to me asking if he might attend a healing session and write a feature for his magazine.

We found that we had much in common. He too was ex-R.A.F. and shared my impatience with the crank fringe associated with psychic matters. George had organised a small group of young healers in his area into a society which he called The Sussex Healers' Association. (This was quite unconnected with the present Sussex Healers' Association, which was founded many years later.) We decided to arrange a series of healing meetings together and share the platform, treating patients alternately. I undertook the organisation of three of these at the Alliance Hall, Westminster, and George arranged three in and around the Brighton area.

We worked well together and it was reassuring to meet someone who, like myself, had discovered his own way in healing. Our methods were curiously similar. It was a brief but harmonious partnership from which, I believe, we both learned a great deal.

These meetings, taking place as they did over a relatively short period of time, attracted the attention of other churches and societies. Letters started to arrive from all over the country, inviting me to conduct similar meetings.

I was certain that if healing were to be accepted as a natural therapy, it must be taken out of its seance-room context and be shown to be perfectly normal and not at all spooky. I therefore welcomed these invitations and threw myself into this public work with great enthusiasm.

One of the first healing meetings I conducted outside London was in Wales. It was well attended and the results were pleasing. After the meeting I was introduced to a middle-aged man who was a local Town Councillor. He was a friendly person and we were soon deep in conversation. It seemed he was a medium, but he did not give sittings professionally. He told me that materialisations regularly happened at his circle.

Physical mediums are extremely rare. Because sittings usually take place in darkness this phenomenon lends itself to fraud more readily than any other psychic manifestation. I had little experience of this form of seance and therefore, when I was invited to attend his circle the following evening, I happily agreed to remain in Wales for an extra day.

The circle met after midnight. They believed that the quieter conditions found in the early hours of the morning permitted a less interrupted contact with the 'other world'. A car was sent to pick me up at 1.30 a.m. to take me to the medium's pleasant home where the meetings were held.

On this occasion there were about ten regular members of the group and three visitors, including myself. Chairs had been arranged in a circle, the medium's chair being larger and resembling a Windsor Wheelback.

There were no trumpets, tambourines, cabinet or other trappings. Because visitors were present, the medium insisted on being roped to his chair so that we might be certain he was not moving about. We were invited to search him and examine the room. Finally, the knots with which he was secured were sealed with wax, so that it would be at once apparent if they were tampered with.

A member of the circle said a short prayer and then we were asked to sing. A red bulb provided sufficient illumination to see everyone quite clearly. The medium was breathing deeply and evenly, as if sleeping. After a while he lifted his head and started to speak in a man's voice which was markedly different from his own normal tones. It was dignified and impressive. After a short explanatory speech the voice requested that we switch out the light and sit for a while in darkness.

There was more singing; but Welsh people sing naturally. After a while, we were instructed by the same voice to switch on the red light. There was a peculiar odour in the room; not unlike the smell of lemon drops or the 'dope' we used to put on the wings of model aeroplanes as children. From the medium's mouth, ears and nose white material appeared to be flowing until it settled in a heap about his feet.

This, I was told, was ectoplasm from which materialisations would draw physical substance to render their spirit bodies solid to our normal senses. It was explained that

66

ectoplasm was composed of particles of energy drawn from everyone present and even from the curtains and fabrics with which the room was furnished. It was able to assume physical substance from chemical charges within the medium's body, where it was first gathered. It all sounded very far-fetched to me.

I was invited to handle the ectoplasm for myself. It looked as though it should feel like muslin. One had heard so much about 'cheese cloth' that the mind automatically expected something of that sort. However, it did not feel like any cloth that I had previously known. The nearest I can come to it is a rubber balloon which has been blown up and then deflated. I held it to my nose and sniffed. There could be no doubt that this was the source of the odour I had detected.

A regular sitter was instructed to hand me one of the thin projections coming from the medium's nose. It appeared soft and pliant in his hands. This, the voice told me, was an 'ectoplasmic rod'. Would I please try to bend it? Although it was no thicker than my finger and I have very strong hands, I could make no impression upon it. As I 'returned' it, the 'rod', which a moment before had been rigid, became as floppy as plasticine. It appeared that the substance was capable of a high degree of control.

The red light was again extinguished and there was a further period of about twenty minutes' singing. A booming voice called for a low light. A much smaller red light was switched on. The medium could be seen dimly, slumped against the ropes which tied him to the chair. He was swathed in great sheets of ectoplasm. Beside his chair, in long white robes, was a figure which we were told was an Ancient Egyptian. It moved among us with apparent freedom, looking quite solid.

It was too good to be true. I had been prepared to accept misty ethereal figures; but this material living person was too much. For about five minutes he chatted with regular members of the circle. They explained to us that the Egyptian was the medium's guide. The light was increased. I could now see the skin of his face and hands. On the back of the hands it was possible to make out small black hairs. His face appeared olive in colour and there was a faint glow about the surface of his skin.

After two or three minutes of the brighter light, he asked for it to be extinguished completely. Once again there was the strong smell that I had noticed was associated with the ectoplasm.

A voice, it sounded like a woman's, asked for light. A dim red light revealed the figure of a small elderly woman — again dressed in white — standing close to the medium. At no time did she move. A visitor said that he believed it to be the form of his mother. She nodded, said a few words to him and then gestured towards the light as if agitated. It was switched off.

She was fairly typical of the twenty or more materialisations which followed. None of them had more than dim light. All were recognised but none by me. All spoke; but seemed capable of only limited communication.

Although there were children among those appearing, I decided that everything we had seen might have been achieved quite easily with the aid of a false door or trap leading under the floor near the medium's chair, two accomplices and a few props, such as white material and wigs — possibly even masks. I determined to search the room more thoroughly than the cursory examination I had made prior to the seance.

I gave the medium full marks for his appraisal of the attitude of his sitters. Everyone, with the exception of myself, had received either a spirit message or at least one materialised figure. Not even the guide had spoken to me directly.

It was 3 a.m. before the circle ended. The 'Egyptian' returned. The light was increased until he asked for a low white bulb. By such illumination it was possible to see gold edging round the white garment which he was wearing. It seemed to be made of silk, and I looked in vain for seams.

He offered up a short prayer and then walked across the room to position himself by the door. I noticed that he was wearing sandals with soft soles and a thong between the toes.

One by one, he called the sitters by their given names and shook them by the hand as he ushered them out of the door — for all the world like a good host saying farewell to his guests. It looked as if, even at this parting ceremony, I was still to be ignored. The room was empty except for myself and the medium — still tied to his chair and breathing deeply — and the carnival figure in fancy robes. I waited to see what would happen next.

"Gordon."

Obediently I walked over to the door and stood in front of him. It was not until then that I realised how tall he was. I am five feet eleven and he was at least six inches taller. Not at all the sort of figure, I would have thought, to be concealed easily under floor boards. He took my hand, clasping it firmly in a warm grasp.

"We brought you nothing," he said. "But were you ready to receive? Let your gift be my blessing."

He gripped my hand so firmly that it hurt. I was unable to release it. Slowly, before my eyes, the tall solid figure collapsed to the floor and melted into a sheet of ectoplasm. The last thing to dissolve was the hand. It ran through my fingers like a thread of elastic, until it joined the whole, became a rod of white, and snaked back to the entranced medium's body.

I did not believe it: but it had happened. Was I hypnotised? I do not think so; but then would one really know? It was a shattering experience. Needless to say, the seals on the ropes were intact and there was no trace of any place where an accomplice might have been concealed.

Some time later, this medium emigrated. His gift attracted attention for many years. I have never heard any report of his being detected in fraud. One feature of his seances was the ability of communicators to talk in their mother tongue; including Swahili, German, Yiddish, Arabic and Chinese. At this type of seance much depends on the ability of the sitters to observe accurately. Even Sir William Crookes, among the most eminent scientists of our age, was accused by his detractors of allowing enthusiasm to sway his judgement.

Deliberate fraud in mediumship is rarer than is generally realised. Self-deception and wishful thinking are much more common. Certainly, physical mediumship is the area of Spiritualism which most easily lends itself to deliberate cheating. Mental mediums, I am sure, frequently delude themselves; but the fraudulent physical medium has to prepare his 'tricks' with malice aforethought.

The worst case of this sort I have come across personally was an ex-telephone engineer who had set himself up as a medium. He employed at least two accomplices, one of whom did preliminary investigations of the sitters, filing the information gathered in a carefully prepared card-index system.

'Spirit voices' were transmitted by radio from a concealed compartment in the seance room. The 'medium' had small speakers concealed in the padding of his jacket. A metal plate, hidden by the thick pile of the carpet, provided the contact when touched by a magnetised connection screwed to the sole of his shoe.

I was invited to sit with this man. Despite an immediate antipathy to him as a person, I was impressed by the 'spirit voices'. In good light, a man and a woman talked with me while the medium was fully conscious and frequently joining in the conversation. No fees were charged, but it was hinted to me, pretty broadly, that any sitters I put their way would be much appreciated and that this might be reflected in some tangible form.

Their technique was to make poor wretches become so involved with their messages, only obtainable through them, that the victims were willing to part with large sums of money — on the advice of their 'loved ones' — so that a centre might be built to further the medium's work.

Finally, it was the Spiritualists who unmasked this vicious confidence trickster. But not before he had raked in about fifty thousand pounds. True to form to the last, he sold his story to a Sunday newspaper before fleeing the country, one step ahead of the police.

Despite the wide publicity he received at the time, he is back in business and my last information was that people are still going to him. He has changed his name, but it is generally known that he is the same fraudulent medium who publicly confessed his guilt.

Among those who have attended his phoney seances since his 'come-back' is a somewhat controversial Bishop of the Church of England.

Once this kind of fraud had been discovered, it is impossible to understand how so-called responsible people can be so credulous as to expose themselves to his deceitful tricks — let alone pay to be cheated!

Chapter VIII

At this time I was receiving about twenty letters a day and answering them personally by hand. On top of everything else, it was a tremendous strain. Funds did not run to a typewriter and my second-hand machine had long since given up the ghost.

Usually, I dealt with this correspondence at night; seldom finishing until two or three in the morning. The strain began to tell. Long hours of working in artificial light inflamed my eyes until I developed corneal ulcers. Foolishly I soldiered on. By the time I agreed to go to Moorfields Eye Hospital, I had to be led across the road.

Somehow, I had to get a typewriter. It was a problem which continuously exercised my mind. In my spare moments I searched second-hand shops, but it was impossible to find anything which might serve my purposes for less than ten pounds — and that might as well have been ten thousand pounds, from the state my finances were in.

One evening I received a telegram which read:
"COME AT ONCE. DOG SERIOUSLY ILL."
The address was a village about twenty miles outside Chester. I checked up that I had enough money for the train fare and wired back the time of my arrival.

The young man who met me at the station could only have been described as exotic. His hair could not have fallen naturally into its beautiful golden curls. I was not able to discuss the purpose of my journey with him as I was too occupied with personal survival. He drove like a bat out of hell. He spread the impress of the powerful car's tyres on every bend of the winding country lanes through which we were travelling. As we went he talked incessantly without stopping to draw breath.

"As we come round the next bend, you'lll see a wall that's been knocked down. That's where I piled the van up last week."

He was one of those endearing drivers who will turn round to talk to their passengers.

"I wish I could have picked you up in the van. It's a converted wartime ambulance with a Humber engine. You should see the way she drifts round these bends. Super!"

With his right hand he felt in his pocket for cigarettes and with his left rummaged in a glove compartment. I wished with all my heart I had remained safely at home. A further dramatic screech from the tyres and we had turned into the drive of an impressive Georgian mansion. Two Afghan hounds gave us a brief, disinterested glance and walked away with superb dignity. Donkeys and goats grazed on what had once been rolling lawns. As the car door slammed there was a crescendo of barking.

Two elderly ladies were at the door to welcome us. Their skirts appeared to have been roughly improvised from old grey woollen blankets and swept the floor as they walked. One of the ladies was smoking a pipe. Both, in my honour, I presume, wore the most incredible Edwardian hats: cherries, peacock feathers, gauze; nothing had been left out.

The interior of the house was a strange mixture of wealth and neglect. Cigarettes had been carelessly stubbed out on superb carpets and furnishings. There were dogs everywhere. Pictures of dogs on the walls, baskets of dogs on the floor, sofas of dogs, chairs of dogs: there must have been at least thirty dogs in the room into which I was ushered.

"Please sit down," said one of the ladies, sweeping a chair clear of a King Charles spaniel. An old mongrel immediately took its place and warned off any further attempt to gain possession.

We perched ourselves on the arms of chairs. Absentmindedly, lady number two knocked out her pipe against an antique bureau. I enquired about my patient.

"We don't really know what is wrong," they told me. "Poor Scabbard won't let anyone into the room. The vet thinks he's gone mad. He has asked us to consider having Scabbard shot. It might be possible for someone to do it from the window."

I followed them upstairs. We walked along a corridor with doors on either side. From every room came excited barking. They sounded like big dogs.

"What sort of dog is Scabbard?" I asked with a rather dry throat.

"An Alsatian. We breed Alsatians, you know. The dogs downstairs are household pets. Our real interest is Alsatians. Scabbard is a champion. One of the best dogs we have ever bred."

We stopped outside a door from behind which came furious growling and rumbling. They looked at me admiringly.

"He's in there," one of them said.

"It must be wonderful to be so trusted by animals," added the other.

I felt trapped. On the one hand I lacked the courage to turn and flee along the corridor and on the other, the prospect of opening that door and loosing the creature making such dreadful sounds, appalled me.

They were still smiling and nodding happily. There was no escape. I grabbed the door handle and pushed the door. As it opened inwards there was a positive roar from within as the dog sprang and pushed it mercifully shut.

"The poor chap seems a little cross," I said fatuously.

"Perhaps if you went in there with him?" one of the ladies suggested. At that moment I positively disliked her.

I took a deep breath and quickly stepped into the room. One of the ladies thoughtfully closed the door behind me.

Scabbard was huge. His size was exaggerated by the way in which every hair on his body was standing on end. He was crouched as if about to spring; his bared teeth looked as big as a piano keyboard. I closed my eyes and waited for the end.

An eternity of minutes dragged by. I opened my eyes. Scabbard had not moved, but I noticed that he was shaking almost as much as I was. Cautiously I moved a few inches. The Alsatian gathered itself for the attack. I froze. There could be no doubt that he really meant it. Because there was no other course of action, I decided to wait it out.

It must have been about thirty minutes before Scabbard moved. Once, a voice from outside enquired if I were all right. The sound agitated the dog so much that it was touch and go for several minutes.

"Shut up!" I hissed, and thank goodness they complied.

At last, the Alsatian struggled to its feet and moved away to the opposite corner of the room. I realised that all was far from well with the animal. I knew it had been forty-eight hours since anyone had been able to give it food and fresh water. But it was more than that which was wrong with the dog.

There was an upright wooden chair in the corner of the room. I walked across and sat on it, deliberately turning it so that I was facing away from Scabbard. There was a further interminable period of waiting. I felt the dog's hot breath on my hand. I kept perfectly still. Something rubbed against my knee. I gave no sign that I had noticed. There was a tiny whimper and a warm tongue touched my hand.

From that point on it was easy. I filled the water bowl from a wash hand basin in the room and Scabbard drank greedily, asking for more when it was empty. I judged it wiser to limit the amount the dog drank until I knew what was wrong. He allowed me to examine him and give him healing. I called the two ladies into the room and suggested they telephone for the vet to come over right away.

I told them that I suspected rat jaundice. (This was later confirmed by the appropriate tests.) I was introduced to the vet. He was cross that I had been called in. Civilly, in my opinion, I offered to muzzle Scabbard while he carried out his examination. He brushed my offer to one side and said that he was capable of handling the dog without assistance, forgetting that he had earlier been talking of shooting the poor beast through the window. When Scabbard bit him, I found it difficult to muster a great deal of sympathy.

Downstairs in the sitting-room again, surrounded by dogs, we sat on the arms of the furniture and munched thick sandwiches. They tried to persuade me to stay the night. There was a spare bed in the room of the exotic young man or, better still, they could erect a camp bed in Scabbard's room. I insisted that I must return home that night.

There was a conference over a train timetable with much shaking of heads. I had missed the last train from Chester; but there was a train which stopped at a station about thirty miles south.

"I'll get you there," said the young man confidently.

I weighted up the various prospects. None of the alternatives was much to my liking.

"Fine. Thank you," I said without much enthusiasm.

As we left, one of the ladies pushed an envelope into my hand.

"That should cover your fare," she told me.

We sped through the night at a pace which made my driver's previous efforts seem like a snail's crawl. Once we came off the road. Unperturbed, he backed the car off the grass verge and resumed our mad journey. Every bump shook us until the car rattled like a load of tin cans.

"That's done the shock-absorbers in," said the exotic young man happily.

He got me to the station with a couple of minutes to spare. I never discovered his relationship to the two elderly ladies.

"That was great fun," he said, as he saw me into a carriage. "We must do it again some time."

I nodded half-heartedly. The train pulled out and I sank wearily back against the cushions. It had been a long day. I felt something unfamiliar in my pocket. I had quite forgotten the envelope. Inside was a cheque for twenty pounds.

And that was how I obtained the money for my much needed typewriter. I bought a reconditioned Continental for seventeen pounds and it gave excellent service for the next fifteen years.

Scabbard lived for a further six years after his recovery from jaundice and won several much-coveted awards.

Chapter IX

The number of patients attending my clinics was growing. Sometimes we continued healing until late into the night. There was a tremendous spirit of pioneering about it all.

Our patients, in the main, were very poor. The way in which they took my small band of young healers to their hearts was deeply moving. We must have seemed callow and inexperienced to these people whose lives were so close to the ultimate realities of life and death. And yet the sanctuary was full of laughter.

I remember two sisters who used to visit us. One was very tall and lugubrious in the extreme; the other was short, plump and full of fun. While they were receiving treatment, the tall sister would do her best to whip up the atmosphere of a religious revival meeting. The jollier half of the duo would join in with an irreverent commentary in the background.

"Lord, I've got faith!" exclaimed the tall one. "I'm 'ealed, I know I'm 'ealed."

"That's right, you tell Him, luv," enjoined her sister.

"I'm going to walk. I know I'm going to walk."

"But you walked in, luv. Don't you remember?"

"Without a limp," glaring at her sister. " 'Cos in Your wisdom You know the carteridge in me left knee 'as gorn an' bust."

"Are you sure it ain't your cartilege, luv?"

" 'E knows! O Gawd, 'e knows!"

" 'Course 'e does, luv. An' if 'e don't, you'll tell 'im," said her sister.

"Stand back! Stand back, everyone! I'm about to take up me bed an' walk. I'm 'ealed! Just as You walked on the water, so I'm goin' ter walk up them steps."

She stood. Her sharp features pinched into a mask of resolution. She charged across the sanctuary, her stick forgotten, and rushed up the four steps leading to the hall. The second step was too much for her and she measured her full length on the floor. There followed a moment of horrified silence. Dishevelled but resolute, she struggled to her feet.

It had all been too much for the jolly sister. Eyes sparkling, she clapped her hands delightedly as she exclaimed:

"Praise be to Gawd! The age of miracles ain't past!"

There is a rich vein of humour in the cockney character.

At this period healers were expected to be able to sense the nature of their patients' ailments without being given any preliminary information. I disliked this practice and discouraged it wherever possible. It seemed to me to be questionable, possibly even dangerous, for people without medical training to offer specialised advice which was outside the normal range of their knowledge. Happily, 'psychic diagnosis' as a preliminary to healing has largely died out.

A taxi-driver's wife attended the clinics who was a delightful Mrs. Malaprop. On her first visit she protested bitterly that she had never been properly 'di-agonised'.

On another occasion she was relating to the waiting patients how much she had enjoyed her first visit to the ballet the previous evening. Not only had the prima-ballerina been presented with a beautiful 'bow-ket', but she had been called back for a 'standing ovulation'. Her best ever was when her husband left her; a not infrequent event in her tempestuous marital relations.

"We've got him now, Mr. Turner," she told me. "I've been to see a solicitor and we're going to sue 'im for the redistribution of conjugal rights."

My circle continued to meet, but our interests were turning from the possibilities of personal psychic development towards research. We tried automatism (writing received through influences outside the conscious mind of the recipient), and I seemed to be particularly receptive to this.

Over a period of six or seven weeks, I received pages of old English script describing events which were purported to have occurred during the reign of Charles II. There was no suggestion that these stemmed from a surviving post-mortal consciousness; but they seemed to originate from a source still believing itself extant.

This script was far neater than my own handwriting. I would take a pen and hold it loosely between my second and third fingers, while the point rested on a blank sheet of paper. It worked best if I were having a conversation with someone on some totally unrelated subject — or even reading a book.

Suddenly, the pen would give a jerk, scribble one or two thin lines, and then it would be off, shooting across the page at least twice as fast as I normally write. I would have someone sitting beside me to pull away the pages as they were completed.

Sometimes my curiosity would get the better of me and I would try to read what was on the paper before the pen had stopped writing. This would inhibit the process or even stop it completely. On one occasion when I tried this, the pen wrote several very rude swear words. And that was the end of the old English script. I often tried to re-establish contact, but I did not seem to have any direct control over the source or type of message which appeared.

These particular communications were vividly detailed, although depressingly sordid. They dealt with the experiences of a man who was suffering from bubonic plague. He was terrified that the filthy old hag who had come to nurse him would murder him for a bag of money tied round his neck. In places these writings resembled the ramblings of a delirious person.

My sanctuary, where these scripts were obtained, was within the area covered by the old City of London where one hundred thousand of its four hundred thousand inhabitants died during the last Black Death epidemic in 1665.

Possibly the events described had taken place in the dwelling which had previously existed on the site. I was at pains to check on the authenticity of some of the colloquialisms in these writings. All appeared to be correct for the period and suggested that the person concerned had been well educated. Certain phrases were peculiar to those used to life on board ship. I was sorry when the scripts stopped. I would have liked to have known the end of the story.

The mysterious substance referred to as ectoplasm fascinated me. The seance I had attended while visiting Wales had made me determined to try to develop some aspect of this phenomenon in my own circle.

I studied the literature on the subject: particularly the writings of Dr. Charles Richet, Dr. Gustave Geley and Sir William Crookes. In theory, ectoplasm was subtle living matter capable of assuming liquid, vaporous or solid states. It extruded through the pores of the body or, in the case of a 'physical medium', through the orifices.

Some researchers had noticed that when ectoplasm assumed physical form the temperature of the seance room was noticeably lowered.

In 1916, Dr. Dombrowski of the Polish Society for Psychical Research had a sample of ectoplasm analysed. The bacteriological report stated: "The substance is albuminoid matter accompanied by fatty matter and cells found in the human organism. Starch and sugar, discoverable by Fehling's Test, are absent."

What I wanted was to find a means of replacing the 'physical medium'. If invisible and vaporous ectoplasm was generated by all the sitters, as the general theory implied, and

81

then gathered and converted in the medium's body, what was the catalyst which enabled this change to take place? I guessed energy — probably some form of electrical energy.

I constructed a 'Heath Robinson' apparatus with which I hoped to test my theory. It was about two feet square, with a long funnel of dark material — intended to replace the 'cabinet' generally used in seances — which I hoped might 'collect' any ectoplasmic emissions. At the end of this funnel was a lighted mirror over an open-cell wet battery.

If the ectoplasm were drawn to the electrical discharge of the battery, it might be visible in the lighted mirror. I used an infra-red bulb to avoid the problem of ectoplasm dissolving in white light. In addition, I sealed a Morse key and buzzer in a glass compartment. This, I felt, should provide the 'spirits' with enough to keep them and us occupied for quite a while.

We sat facing the 'ectoplasm box' and everyone was provided with a pencil and notebook to jot down anything he might see or hear. It was a rule that no-one should speak; thus avoiding the problem of suggestion. Otherwise, we followed the familiar pattern of all seance circles. To 'build up the power' we sang or used a gramophone to supplement our vocal efforts. We limited the duration of each seance to one hour.

Nothing occurred for several weeks. Our first 'happening' was not directly connected with the apparatus I had provided. There was a patter of light raps from different parts of the room.

"God bless you, friend," everyone said delightedly.

"Shut up!" I rejoined firmly. "Write it down."

The 'ectoplasm box' was placed on a sideboard against the wall. Its red light illuminated the room fairly adequately. Particularly, it lighted a print hung about three feet above it. On the night of the raps this picture started to swing a few inches from side to side. Everyone noted the fact on his pad.

Within a few weeks the print was swinging vigorously in

time with our singing. We all noted a grey mist gathering in the apparatus and the buzzer was pressed on three occasions. We were terribly excited and increased the frequency of our sittings to twice a week.

The grey mist started to shape into more solid forms. Usually these were faces, but occasionally there would be a complete picture, such as a simple scene as on a photograph or Christmas card. It was obvious from notes made by members of the circle that these were seen objectively. Our 'ectoplasm box' was given a new title. We called it our 'spirit television'.

A young interior decorator was so grateful for the healing of his back that he completely redecorated the room in which we held our seances. I told him about the phenomena we had been getting and he expressed his scepticism in no uncertain terms.

"Somebody's been pulling your leg, mate," he told me. "You let me come along with my friend who is an amateur conjurer. We'll soon sort out what's going on."

"Fair enough," I replied. "Come tomorrow."

The conjurer gave us a long dissertation about all mediums being fraudulent. He knew all their tricks. Nobody would ever put anything over on him. He glared at us meaningfully.

He practically dismantled the apparatus. So thorough was his examination, that we were nearly two hours late starting. Once the music started it was no time at all before the picture was swinging happily from side to side. The buzzer joined in and there was a volley of light taps.

Suddenly there was the crash of a chair being overturned as its occupant leapt to his feet. The amateur conjurer was shaking like an aspen, his hair standing on end.

"Blimey!" he said, and with that he bolted. The decorator followed hard on his heels.

My 'spirit television' seemed to provide an answer to many of the problems of mediumship. I was convinced that I had stumbled upon a tremendous discovery. Alas, it did not prove to be quite so simple. One night there was nothing. No raps, no sounds from the buzzer, no grey mist: even the picture refused to move.

"Never mind," I thought. "Next time it will work."

But, although we persisted, we were unable to reproduce the earlier results. In the twelve years that our circle met we experienced every form of psychic phenomenon; but it was always transient and never remained the same for more than a few months at a time.

Chapter X

At about this time I received a letter inviting me to undertake a short healing tour of the Yorkshire mining villages. The idea was to present two healing meetings a day. The organiser was sure he could successfully arrange thirteen in seven days. Most miners worked shift-work and this meant it was possible to draw audiences in the afternoon as well as in the evening. I had been over-working for many months, but I agreed to undertake this marathon without a second thought. New ideas had always appealed to me.

The organiser, Jim, was an ex-miner. He met me at Doncaster Station, wearing a cloth cap and a greasy mackintosh. He was a little man with sharp, shrewd features.

He regarded me with some suspicion.

"You're a mite young and a bit pasty for my liking," he observed. "But if you can do the job, you'll do. Us'll see before too long, no doubt."

He led me out of the station and over to an enormous motor-bike. It must have been manufactured about the time of the 1914-18 war. A pillion had been improvised from an even greasier raincoat than the one he was wearing. On the back of the bike an L-plate had been tied. I felt distinctly uneasy.

At the best of times I have very little affection for motor-cycles. This one was a brute. Jim drove the thing fairly sedately, but when we reached the cobbled streets of the little villages, we bounced about all over the place. It was like trying to ride a bucking horse. I clutched my suitcase and closed my eyes. Time and again my bottom lost all contact with the rock solid pillion.

Eventually we came to a village called Grimethorpe. It was

made up of row upon row of black terraced cottages. Old men squatted on their hunkers outside the front doors. Their rheumy eyes followed our progress, but their faces betrayed no expression. Every street seemed to be a steep hill. Notices warned: "Beware of Subsidence".

We pulled up at an end cottage. Jim pushed his bike to a little passage beside the house and stored it in the small garden. The back of the place was even more daunting than the front. An open drain ran along the centre of a narrow cobbled lane which divided the back of one street from the next.

In the distance one could see the big wheels of the colliery pithead. A huge heap of slag pointed a black finger to the sky. Jim followed the direction of my gaze.

"Makes a pretty sight wi' the sunset be'ind, does that. You've got nowt like that in Lunnon, I'll be bound. Tha'd better come in an' meet Bertha. She's no oil painting, but she'll look after yer while yer 'ere." He gestured towards the back door.

Bertha was cooking at a coal-fired range. As Jim had so eloquently expressed it, she was no oil painting. The politest description might have been 'Junoesque'. Her massive red arms resembled whole hams. She looked as if she could make two of Jim and would at the drop of a hat.

He introduced me and she acknowledged my presence with a curt nod.

"If he's come all t'way from Lunnon, he'll be needing tay. Don't stand there gawping, tha knows where t'kettle is." Jim jumped to it, as if commanded by a sergeant major.

She addressed me directly for the first time.

"Does tha know what subsidence is?"

"No."

"It means they built the 'ouses on top o' the coalpits. So t'ground's falling away. That's what those cracks down t'wall are. If it starts creaking in t'night, don't worry — it won't

86

tumble down yet awhile. We've no gas, no electric and toilet's out back. All the comforts of 'ome, like. 'Appen tha'll 'ave to put up wi't while tha'rt 'ere."

Jim chipped in: "Does t'a take tay in cup or mug?"

He was regarding me so intently, that I realised this must be a very important question. I took a chance.

"A mug will be fine, thank you," I said.

Jim filled a pint mug with tea, added tinned condensed milk and two large spoonfuls of sugar and handed the concoction to me. It was the colour of brown boot polish.

"Tha'll do," he said. "Aye, tha'll do." And with that I was accepted into the bosom of the family.

We dined on pigs' trotters and baked beans: a combination of flavours which I have never repeated and the memory of which remains with me even after twenty years.

Our repast completed, Bertha handed me a stone hot water bottle, and I climbed the narrow stairs to my room. I pulled back the bedcovers and slipped the bottle between the sheets. At first I thought it must have started a fire, but on investigation discovered that what had looked like smoke was in fact steam. I put my raincoat between the bottom sheet and the mattress and climbed into bed, hoping that youth and faith would protect my kidneys from irreparable harm.

It was difficult to sleep. The cottage creaked and groaned as the earth beneath it subsided. A mouse started to chew at the ceiling over my bed. The creature sounded hungry and determined. I could hear the low murmur of the voices of my host and hostess coming from the room below.

After a while they climbed the stairs and I could hear them moving about in the room next to mine. The dividing wall could only have been a thin partition for their voices were embarrassingly clear.

"And you get 'im a decent breakfast in the morning, you lazy old cow," said Jim. "I were right ashamed of supper t'night. By the 'eck! What sort of food is bloody pigs' feet, fer a man from Lunnon?"

" 'E'll eat same as us an' like it," replied Bertha. " 'Oo the
'ell does 'e think 'e is anyway that 'e can't eat trotters? Tha
wants to go to work an' earn a few bob, then we could afford
to entertain oop to Lunnon standards."

They carried on in this vein for about half an hour, their
voices growing louder and angrier with every exchange. It was
hard to judge who delivered the first blow. The second, third,
fourth and fifth certainly belonged to Bertha. This was clear
from Jim's shrieks. I thought of the massive arms and
shuddered.

The ultimate reconciliation was a lengthy process; but
obviously satisfying to both contestants.

The next morning Jim woke me with a mug of tea. One of
his eyes was red and swollen.

"I tripped on me way to t'privvy," he told me. "You've
got ter be careful o' that in t'dark. Bertha's boiling oop a
kettle. Tha can shave in t'kitchen when th'art ready."

I shaved while Bertha fried eggs and bacon for breakfast,
carefully refraining from asking whether she had sustained
her cut lip in an accident similar to Jim's.

"Tha can wait in t'parlour when th'art ready," said Bertha.
"Don't mind t'bitch. She's a bit niggly while she's still
suckling her pups."

In the parlour in front of a blazing fire was a brown and
white terrier-type mongrel bitch. She eyed me suspiciously.
At the 'milk bar' were eight fat puppies. I went over and
made friends. She allowed me to take one of the pups and
play with it on my lap. Jim walked in bearing a dish of bacon
and eggs.

"I'll just put these in front o' t'fire to keep 'ot," he said.
"An' you leave them alone," he said to the dog. "You touch
those and I'll beat you pups or no pups." From the way she
cringed it was apparent that he meant it.

Playing with the pup, my attention was distracted from

the bitch. I heard the sound of licking. She had lifted one of the eggs off the plate and was gently licking it. By a miracle it was not broken. I pushed her away and slipped it back onto the plate.

As Bertha served the eggs and bacon, I watched with bated breath. In her basket, the bitch was happily cleaning her pups. I considered saying I did not eat eggs, but the pigs' trotters had not been very sustaining and I was hungry. The licked egg was deposited on Jim's plate. He attacked it with relish.

"Eh!" he exclaimed. "Though I say it as shouldn't, Bertha fries a good egg."

During the morning I treated patients in the small parlour and after lunch left on the pillion of Jim's motorbike for my first healing meeting. It was to be held in a Miners' Institute from which a local Spiritualist group had rented a room.

The cases were mostly very serious. Disseminated sclerosis and silicosis seemed prevalent. After the meeting, I remained behind to treat as many patients as possible before going on to the second meeting.

A little girl of seven was brought to me. She had been involved in an accident which had damaged her spine. With the aid of leg irons and arm crutches, she could walk a few paces, but only with great difficulty. She was such a pretty child.

I removed the irons and gently massaged her legs. They were badly wasted and very thin. I ran the tips of my fingers down her spine. At one spot they stopped and vibrated rapidly. Without conscious volition my fingers paused on one of the vertebrae. It moved. They passed on to another and that also shifted. The child was smiling and chattering happily.

"Try and stand without your crutches, darling," I said.

She stood. I deliberately kept my voice casual.

"Walk a step or two. It's quite easy."

89

The child walked. Her legs were weak and none too steady. But she was walking without irons or crutches. Her tearful mother promised to encourage the child to exercise the muscles of her legs, and she left bearing crutches and irons in her arms.

And so the tour went on. Jogging through the narrow streets on Jim's ancient bike, we had capacity crowds wherever we went. One feature of these Yorkshire meetings was the church teas.

At every church we visited they would have a massive tea party before the meeting. Chairs would be pushed back and long trestle tables spread with cakes, sausage rolls and sandwiches. It was nothing to sit down three hundred people for tea. Everything was home baked by the members.

For me, these teas represented sheer purgatory. At the best of times I am clumsy. My wife goes further and describes me as 'accident prone'.

They would put a cup and saucer in one hand and a plate in the other.

"Now you must have one of Mrs. Clutterbuck's sausage rolls and one of these watercress sandwiches, made by Mrs. Postlethwaite. What about a slice of this lovely seed cake made by Mrs. Dogood, our organist?"

They would load me with cakes, sandwiches — the lot. They would fill my plate, put them between my fingers and balance them on my saucer, until I looked like a bad juggler at a third rate cabaret. Then they would say firmly:

"You must meet Mrs. Shufflebottom, our President. She's dying to shake hands with you."

With that a stout overdressed woman would advance towards me with hand outstretched. I would look for somewhere to deposit my load. Every available surface would be smothered with plates of goodies. In desperation I would try to transfer everything to my left hand.

Crash!

Sudden awful silence. Feebly, I would try to pick up bits of broken teacup and sodden seed cake. The President's smiling face would change to a frozen mask.

"Don't you worry about that, Mr. Turner. Someone fetch him another cup and saucer. Perhaps it would be better to give him one of the plain white ones this time. Don't give it another thought. It were an old one anyway. That service were given to me by my grandmother on my wedding day. That were fifty years ago and I've still got the complete set. At least, I 'ad until just now. But don't you give it a second thought."

Another variant of this form of sadism was for them to wait until I had bitten into a watercress sandwich and bits of greenery were hanging from the corners of my mouth. And then they would pounce on me with the inevitable question:

"Now, tell me, Mr. Turner. How did you first discover you had a healing gift?"

On my Yorkshire tour I sometimes had to face two of these teas a day. Somehow, I survived. Just as I survived Jim's motorbike; although on one occasion it was a very close thing.

We were late for our second meeting and Jim was flogging the life out of his ancient machine. Suddenly the front tyre burst. There was a lorry coming in the opposite direction. Jim went into the ditch and I was thrown in the path of the oncoming vehicle.

In the R.A.F., I once took a parachute jumping course. We were taught how to roll off the back of a truck travelling at thirty miles per hour. I hated the course which I had to terminate through vertigo — although this had never troubled me when I was flying.

My subconscious mind must have assimilated more of this training than I had realised. I went into a perfect parachute landing roll which carried me safely clear of the lorry's wheels. Apart from bruises and a small tear in my trousers, there was no damage to either of us.

We hitched a lift and arrived at the hall with a minute or two to spare. Halfway through the meeting reaction set in. I started to tremble from head to toe.

At the end an old lady walked up to me.

"That were marvellous," she said. "You've got a wonderful gift. Do you know, there were so much power on that platform, I could see you shaking with it."

The climax of the tour was an afternoon meeting at a little village named Cudworth and pronounced, for some reason, Cud'oth. It had been arranged that I demonstrate healing in the Miners' Club. In the evening I was to speak at the Harvest Festival in the local church.

At the start of the healing, I rashly said I would remain behind until everyone who had come for treatment had been seen. During the meeting a woman suffering from diabetic blindness recovered her sight.

Word spread like a forest fire. The hall had capacity seating for one hundred and fifty people. More than three hundred jammed their way in. They brought the sick from miles around. A newspaper reporter stood up and challenged me on my promise.

"What about your assurance that you will treat everybody who has come to receive healing?" he asked in a snide tone.

"It stands," I replied.

As fast as I treated them the hall filled up with more sick people. I was still working at one in the morning when they finally had to close the hall. I had been healing for ten hours without a break.

Suddenly it dawned on me. I had clean forgotten the Harvest Festival. I started apologising to Jim for my thoughtlessness.

"Don't you worry," he told me. "They're still waiting for thee. I told 'em tha'd come when tha'd finished."

The church was packed with more sick people. They had

been waiting since six-thirty the previous evening. As I walked in they clustered round me asking for healing.

"Blow the service!" I said. "I'm going to treat these people."

When I finished four hours later, I ate some food and passed out from exhaustion. Jim and Bertha had to carry me upstairs to bed.

I woke eight hours later, to find myself a local celebrity. A queue of people was waiting outside hoping I might treat them.

After a wash and shave, I was forced to obey a call of nature. I made my way out to the lean-to in the back yard, much to my embarrassment having to pass the line of waiting people.

It was a temporary structure of corrugated iron built by Jim to house an old Elsan chemical lavatory. As I sat down my elbow caught one of the walls. There was a creaking noise and the whole thing collapsed outwards. I was revealed sat in regal state, to the delight of the queue.

One old collier lifted his flat cap and gave me a broad wink.

" 'Ow do," he called.

I clutched my trousers to me and fled.

Bertha packed my suitcase to enable me to continue healing until the very last moment, and then I was bumping along on the back of Jim's motorbike — fortunately it was undamaged by our spill.

At Doncaster Station a small crowd had gathered to see me off. They presented me with flowers and a white canary in a cage. But they had one special surprise. They pointed to the far end of the platform where a little girl was standing with her mother. She ran to greet me. As I leant forward to receive her, she threw her arms round my neck and kissed me.

It was the child I had treated at the first meeting with the leg irons and arm crutches.

I wept for joy.

Jim patted me on the shoulder.

"Tha'll do, lad," he said as he bundled me into a compartment.

Chapter XI

The winter of 1952 was very cold. On the London pavements snow lingered in ugly grey heaps. For me it was a time of ill health. First it was influenza and then tonsilitis. For several days I was delirious. Inadequate nutrition and overwork had lowered my resistance.

Being a healer does not absolve one from the responsibility of caring for one's own health. This was a lesson I was slow to learn. Always there was a driving compulsion to get back to my patients as quickly as possible. It is surprising how often we repeat the same mistakes over and over again.

I had to discontinue my active interest in sport — Judo and Rugby football — as undue exertion caused severe pain in my chest. Even climbing the stairs left me breathless. I hoped that if I ignored the symptoms they would go away: in the meantime, I continued to overwork.

Shortly after Christmas, I was alone in the house, working on a backlog of letters, when I heard the telephone ringing in the hall three floors below. As I ran downstairs, I felt a searing pain like a steel vice gripping my chest. I regained consciousness a few minutes later.

I must have fallen down the last flight of stairs. My chest was sore, almost as if I had been punched. I felt dreadful.

The doctor whom I consulted was a Pole. He knew about my healing and was sympathetic to my ideas. From time to time he had even sent patients to my clinic.

He examined me thoroughly and shook his head.

"I have no doubt that you have suffered a heart attack. You must go into hospital at once. Proper tests must be carried out to ascertain the extent of the damage. Is there a history of heart illness in your family?'

And so I had inherited more from my mother than her psychic faculty: the weak heart, so prevalent in her family, was to be mine too.

I refused to go into hospital, not because I disagreed with orthodox medical treatment, but because the slender finances of my sanctuary were so precariously balanced that I was afraid that my prolonged absence would prove disastrous.

It was all too obvious that I must rest. Therefore, when Doris and Bill asked me to stay with them in their Battersea flat, I accepted with alacrity. On the first evening I suffered a further small heart incident. I was ordered to bed and it was a month before I was strong enough to resume my healing.

I returned to the sanctuary only to find that we had been ordered to close. The lady who rented the house had granted me permission to use her cellar, but had neglected to inform her landlord. He had found out about my work through newspaper accounts. The key lease expressly forbade professional use. He gave me seven days to quit.

It seemed like the end of my world. But once again Doris and Bill came to the rescue by offering their flat until I could find somewhere else. In addition, I arranged to hire the Cooperative Hall in Seven Sisters Road, North London, on two evenings a week, so that the patients who had been visiting my sanctuary would have a place close at hand.

Closing down the little cellar sanctuary on which we had worked so hard and which had served us so well, was very sad. Our final healing session was packed and we worked late into the night to treat the queue of waiting people.

It had been my intention to hire the hall only for as long as it took to complete the treatment of patients who had been visiting my previous sanctuary. In fact, the work expanded to such a degree that I continued there for eight years.

The main hall seated two hundred people. But there were five smaller halls and we started with one of these. It was situated in a tough area. During the time we were there a policeman was stabbed to death outside the adjoining dance hall, and a youth was stabbed in the stomach in an amusement arcade on the opposite side of the street.

I used the flat in Battersea for about three months and then found a house to rent in Thurleigh Road close to Wandsworth Common. I was able to split the rent with Bill, who took over half the house. It was an excellent arrangement which worked very well for the next ten years.

There was sufficient space to provide me with a large ground floor sanctuary and waiting room, as well as a study at the top of the house.

Working in my new sanctuary, my health improved and the volume of work multiplied. Soon, I was conducting five clinics every week in South London as well as two in North London.

More healers joined me and we organised ourselves as a society which we called the Fellowship of Healing. Our Committee — if that word can be applied — was composed of the original members of my circle. As new healers joined us they automatically attended the circle and had a voice in affairs.

Throughout all this time I had continued my study and practice of meditation. I found Zen an intractable pathway. Its abstractions were too difficult for my Western mind to grasp.

I was increasingly drawn to the use of colour and symbols as aids to concentration. Gradually, a system emerged which served my needs, both as an aid to attunement and as a means of quietening my over-active mind. Today, it has been estimated that more than twenty thousand people are using my method of 'meditation through three-fold attunement'.

Meditation helped me with absent or distant healing. Every day I received letters from all over the world asking me to heal patients at a distance. This involved mental attunement with people about whom I might have no more information than their names and addresses and the complaints from which they were suffering.

When I had first started absent healing it was then common practice to read out a list of names and addresses each night at an appointed time. This was believed to transmit the information to post-mortal healers who then visited the patient and carried out the healing.

I could not believe wholeheartedly in this technique. There seemed to me to be something doubtful about the whole process. One healer claimed to have more than ten thousand people on his list. With all the goodwill in the world, it was impossible for me to believe that he could give personal attention to such a vast host of patients.

Some years later I discovered how this huge postbag was dealt with. Standard replies were drafted; one for patients who were showing signs of progress and another for those who were not improving. These replies were changed at least twice a week. The whole operation was as organised as the football pools or a mail order business.

There was a machine to sign the notepaper and another to open envelopes. Letters were dealt with by outworkers who were supplied with a long list of questions and answers so that they might draft their replies around the stock letters.

Despite this there were some positive results — although I very much doubt if the percentage of success was anything like as high as has been claimed. Such cures took place without the healer even reading the patient's letter, possibly without his even knowing of its existence.

My own absent healing has always been personal. If I were to receive more letters than I could myself read, I would feel forced to curtail this aspect of my work. It is astonishing the way people will pour out their troubles to an absolute stranger. So many of the letters I receive are a cry from the heart. I always try to remember this in my replies to patients.

"Dear Gordon Turner," a patient wrote. "My husband is dying of cancer. He is in St. Stephen's Hospital and there is nothing more that can physically be done. We have been married for eleven years and love each other as much now as on our wedding day. If my husband is beyond healing — as I believe he is — please try to help him to die quickly, so he does not suffer."

The letter was similar to many others I had received, but something about it touched me deeply. During my absent healing attunement, I felt very close to the dying man. As I prepared for bed I continued to think about him.

That night I had a vivid dream. I was in a small hospital ward which contained about eight beds. In the second bed on my left was a man of about forty. He was desperately thin. There was an oxygen cylinder beside his bed. As he gulped each fresh breath there was a rasping sawing sound.

I stood at the foot of his bed. His eyes were open. He managed to nod slightly as if in recognition. Somehow, I knew he was my patient. I moved to the side of his bed and placed my hands on his chest. I am always conscious of an energy flowing through me when I am giving healing treatment; but this was far more intense than I had ever previously experienced.

Drops of liquid colour seemed to run from my fingers. Gold, blue, silver and mauve; they ran into the sick man's chest in a constant stream. From the palms of my hands came shafts of similarly coloured light.

After a short while, his chest seemed to glow with a soft white phosphorescent light. I was intensely aware of the malignant illness beneath my hands. It was as if a foul parasite had invaded his body.

The glow increased and expanded until it appeared to be a replica of his body, floating several inches above its physical counterpart. Both 'bodies' were now sleeping. I stood back knowing that my part in his healing was now complete.

Two days later I received a letter from his wife telling me that he had died peacefully during the night of my dream: this despite the fact that she had been told that his ordeal might be protracted over several days.

I started to experiment on using mental directives to guide healing during sleep, until it became an integral part of my system of distant healing. Over the years there have been many examples of people being aware of my presence and even young children describing "the man who came and stood beside my bed".

1953 was a year of intense activity. Principally I remember it for one person — John Britnell. Healers in Britain were beginning to organise themselves. John had started an Essex Healers' Association which had attracted more than three hundred members; although some of them resided outside the County boundaries. Under his influence Albert Ellis had started an East Midlands Association and I started the Surrey and South London.

John looked forward to the day when there would be a National Society. We talked the idea over for hours. Healers must unite to achieve professional status. If this were to be done there must be an organisation which could speak for them. We hoped it might be possible also to provide an insurance cover which would protect patients against negligence. The lack of such a scheme gave rise to one of the most frequent attacks launched on unqualified practitioners.

It was difficult to foresee a time when healers would be able to sit professional examinations; but if this were not possible, we could at least do our best to ensure that those setting themselves up as healers were of suitable character and background. Gradually, there began to emerge a skeleton of the type of association we needed.

Britnell was a retired postal worker. He had been awarded the British Empire Medal for his work in setting up an efficient First Aid training scheme within the Post Office. He was a very useful healer and an indefatigable organiser; but his sphere of influence tended to be regional.

I agreed to return to the North to try to organise a Yorkshire Healers' Association. This time I undertook twenty-three meetings in fourteen days. Everywhere I went I enlisted the support of local healers. I returned to London with an association founded with more than one hundred members.

A factor which spurred us to a sense of urgency was that the Archbishop of Canterbury had convened a Commission to report on Divine Healing. We were not to know that it would be five years before this report was to be published; or that the Commission would duck its responsibility for coming out either for or against the efficacy of healing. By deeming the consideration of such evidence as outside their terms of reference, they neatly side-stepped the one issue which was crucial to the whole report.

We called ourselves the National Federation of Spiritual Healers. John Britnell was the first Chairman and I was Public Relations Officer and Vice-Chairman. Harry Edwards was invited to be the first President. Four of us had met at John Britnell's home in Goodmayes, Essex, and set our signatures to a minute recording its foundation. We represented more than five hundred healers. It was quite an occasion — or so it seemed to us.

John favoured the name British Association of Spiritual Healers. I pointed out that these initials spelt BASH. If I had known some of the wrangles which were to occur in succeeding years I might have thought this not inappropriate. As it was, my suggestion of National Federation of Spiritual Healers was unanimously adopted. It was also my recommendation that we should consult barrister Percy Wilson to draw up a draft constitution. In the event, much of the work was carried out by his son Laurie, also an eminent barrister.

Chapter XII

Healing was coming into fashion and with it came the interest of fashionable journalists. Beverley Nichols wrote several articles followed by a book on the subject. Although I did not know Beverley at that time, he was later to come to me as a patient.

I was approached by Paul Bretherton, a journalist working on the *Sunday Dispatch*. Godfrey Winn — possibly the most famous columnist in Britain at that time — was to carry out an investigation of healing. Winn wanted to write about my work — particularly with animals — and the *Dispatch* would be grateful for any advice and help I might be able to give him. This investigation was to be published as a series of articles in the *Sunday Dispatch* and later, in extended form, as a book entitled *Quest for Healing*.

An appointment was made for Winn to visit me. I was not enamoured of his emotive style of journalism, but in the climate of that time, I was in favour of any form of publicity which might bring healing to the attention of a wider audience. Winn was read by millions, therefore I was prepared to do my best to assist his inquiries.

I do not know quite what I expected. Certainly the meeting could never be described as an outstanding success. He made it obvious from the start that he felt an instant antipathy. He would ask questions and then interrupt me before I could say more than two or three words.

"Now tell me, Mr. Turner, how did you first discover you were a healer?"

"That's not easy to answer in a few words. I suppose it was something I always knew. When I was a boy . . ."

"Don't tell me your life story, just answer my question."

"I'm trying to."

"How do you imagine your healing power works?"

"I have given that a lot of thought . . ."

"Then don't bother with the question, it would take too long."

I felt like chucking him out on his ear. He seemed to me the most conceited person it had ever been my misfortune to meet. What I did not know was that Winn was under terrible strain. His mother, whom he adored, was dying. For weeks, he had watched this, hoping for a miracle. He wanted to believe in healing, but feared that he might not be able to bear the disappointment if it were to fail.

His doctor had ordered him to rest from the strain of this vigil. He went to Madeira where he became acquainted with an American, W. J. MacMillan, who was enjoying a considerable vogue, following the publication of his book, *The Reluctant Healer.* Winn felt that this meeting with 'Mac' was more than chance. And yet he still hung back. What if it failed? Instinctively he knew that his mother had passed beyond the stage where even healing could save her.

On his return to England, the *Sunday Dispatch,* to which he was then under contract, proposed that he write a series of articles under the group title 'Faith Healing, Fact or Fiction?'. Winn did not want to face up to the personal implications of such an investigation. In fact, it was he who was to prove 'The Reluctant Reporter'.

I was invited to visit the News Room at the Dispatch offices to discuss the series with a reporter named Donald Dynsley, whose father had been one of Fleet Street's best known crime reporters. 'Dyn' was a splendid chap, and we remained friends for many years.

At our first meeting Dynsley was sceptical about healing. One of his colleagues had a 'frozen shoulder' which was locked so that he could not lift his arm. I was invited to test my 'powers'. The hesitant victim was placed on a chair in the middle of the News Room with a crowd of grinning reporters gathered round.

The minute I placed my hands on it, I knew it would be all right. I waited a moment or two until I could feel it moving freely under my fingers and then took the wrist and lifted the arm effortlessly to its full height. No one was more surprised than the reporter who was healed. Following this instant success, my relationship with 'Dyn' and the other reporters became extremely cordial.

But between Winn and me there blew an Arctic wind as freezing as any that had blunted the tips of his fingers with frost-bite. For Winn was a courageous man. During the Second World War he sailed on a destroyer in the dreadful Arctic convoys and was the first journalist to parachute into Norway during the struggle for its liberation.

It was arranged that I should accompany Winn on his visit to Harry Edwards' sanctuary in Surrey. His car was to call for me at 10 a.m. and we would drive down together and have lunch with Edwards before attending his healing session in the afternoon.

Winn arrived just before 11.00. He was in a foul mood.

"My shoulder is hurting. My chauffeur has given it a massage but it is still sore. You had better try some of your healing on it," he complained.

He removed his jacket and I put my hand on his shoulder. Before I could achieve anything he jumped up.

"Haven't you finished yet?"

"I haven't even started yet," I said as calmly as the circumstances permitted.

"Well, we can't hang about here all day. I've got an appointment to keep." He stamped out of the house and climbed into the car beside his chauffeur.

I sat in the back.

They chatted away happily, pointedly ignoring my presence. We stopped three times. Twice for sherry and the third because Winn saw some attractive leaves in a hedgerow.

104

"We must gather some of those too, too beautiful colours for Mother!" he exclaimed.

With the aid of the chauffeur, he gathered prodigious quantities of undergrowth which they thrust into the back of the car, without the slightest regard for my person. I peeped out from between the leaves like a Japanese sniper and smouldered.

On our arrival at Harry Edwards' imposing home, Winn's manner changed completely. He was courtesy itself. I introduced them and tried to melt into the background.

The initial formalities dispensed with, Winn opened the bidding.

"I believe you know my dear friend Sir John —?"

Edwards hesitated for only a fraction of a second.

"That's right. He came to me through Lord and Lady —."

"Of course, dear Simon and Elizabeth," beamed Winn. "I saw them only recently when I was visiting Baroness —."

For all his smile his eyes were saying, 'your bid!'.

By the time Edwards brought play to a close with two princesses and a duke, we had worked our way through a sizeable chunk of Debrett's and earned our lunch.

Afterwards, we sat through the healing session. Winn made a few brief notes and talked to one or two people. He seemed interested in a guarded sort of way; but I felt that he was not putting himself out to make a very thorough examination of the material made available to him.

We had tea and Edwards bade us a cordial farewell. I climbed back among the shrubbery with which the rear of the car was festooned. For several miles we drove in silence. The chauffeur was the first to speak.

"What did you make of him, Sir?"

Winn's reply was a sneer.

"He started out as a printer, I understand. Despite all of that," he waved back in the general direction of Harry Edwards' grounds, "he is still a printer, as far as I am concerned."

I was livid. I had put up with a lot that day, but this was the last straw.

"If it weren't for printers," I said, "there would be no-one to print your awful articles and you wouldn't be riding in this ruddy great car!"

There was a frightful silence. Winn's neck started to swell over his collar and change from a pleasant tan to red and then puce.

"And furthermore, I can remember another pretty good healer who started life by being only a carpenter," I added.

From the front of the car there was a hissing sound as of someone winded. We completed the journey in silence. They dropped me at my front gate and we parted with icy farewells.

The next day 'Dyn' telephoned.

"What the hell have you been doing to Godfrey? He has told Charles Eade (then editor of the *Dispatch*) that he doesn't want you to have anything further to do with the series and he won't write about your work."

"Jolly good!" I said, and meant it.

Godfrey Winn's series turned out to be extremely fair. I would go further; I think it was the most mature coverage of healing to appear in a national paper up to that time. True, there had been many articles on individual healers; but Winn's series was far better researched and spread across a wider area.

Towards the end of the series Winn wrote me a civil note thanking me for the help I had given him and asking if he might visit a healing session for animals. His subsequent article was sympathetic and provided the substance of a chapter in his book.

In the ensuing years, I came to know Godfrey quite well. We shared public platforms on several occasions and for a while we were close neighbours.

One night I called into a bistro near my London

106

pied-à-terre. Godfrey was the only other customer and so we shared a table. He spoke of the mental agony he suffered during that time. His true quest had been for a cure for his mother.

Chapter XIII

Shortly after my move to South West London I became involved in an attempt to 'exorcise' a poltergeist. The phenomena occurred in a Battersea shop. The family living in the flat above had an adolescent daughter — a factor common to most hauntings of this type.

It was reported that after the shop was vacated in the evenings banging noises and sounds resembling a heavy bolt being drawn had been heard. In one room objects had been thrown including a framed picture which had flown from one end to the other, smashing the glass. Witnesses were certain that nobody had been close to it when it had happened.

My first examination of the shop was in daylight. Despite adequate heating and ventilation, the place felt damp and cold. There was a faint odour of decay, and I sensed that I was unwelcome. People who worked there described a feeling of unaccountable fear which suddenly gripped them. I knew what they meant.

I arranged an all night 'vigil seance' with a few friends. What had seemed mildly unpleasant by daylight was positively frightening by night. We started with a tour of the premises. Half-way round we heard the distinct sound of a bolt being drawn. It seemed to come from the street door in a room we had just left. We hurried back. A roll of toilet paper was stretched across the room as if it had been thrown. It had not been there two minutes before. The bolt was still firmly in position.

As this room seemed to be the centre-point for the haunting we decided to hold our seance there. We arranged a small circle of chairs and waited. Almost at once there was a flurry of agitated bangs and raps. We sat in darkness except for faint moonlight filtering through a single small frosted window. It was an eerie enough setting for any ghost hunt.

At this point I lost touch with the story for a while and had to rely on what I was later told by the others. It seemed that for a few minutes I breathed deeply and then passed into a deep trance. From my point of view, this felt exactly like being anaesthetised.

While I was in this state a woman's voice came from my lips and ordered my friends to leave. She appeared to believe they were intruders who had forced their way into her home. She refused to believe that she might be in some sort of post-mortal state despite efforts to dissuade her.

Every attempt to reason with her failed and she finally 'vacated' her position to an elderly man. He appeared physically deformed and my body was twisted into the contours of a hunchback. Using my body as if it were his own, he rose to his feet and shuffled out of the room. The people forming the circle carefully got up and followed. He entered a small concrete-floored room, lay full length on the floor and crossed his arms on his chest. It was in this position that I regained consciousness.

I later discovered that this shop had at one time been occupied by an undertaker. The room in which the 'twisted spirit' stretched out on the floor had been used as a small chapel where the bodies were kept prior to burial.

For a brief while this shop was the scene of one of the most virulent hauntings I have ever known. It was as if it had become a 'psychic pocket' which provided energy for the manifestations. Suddenly the phenomena stopped as unaccountably as they had started.

One evening I was walking around these premises at about 7 p.m. The people who worked there had left and all seemed quiet. I became aware of a curious scratching sound from the room I was about to enter. My first thoughts were not of the supernatural. I flung open the door expecting to find a rat or somebody trying to force a window.

What in fact I saw came as a complete surprise. I was able to observe it for at least a full minute. I had never seen anything like it before nor have I since. It was about three feet six inches tall and completely black. Its head was like a long curved beak and the eyes glowed red as burning embers. It had a humanoid body with small hands and feet. I think that the hands had only three fingers, but of this I could not be completely certain.

While I stood rooted to the spot regarding this strange apparition, it stood perfectly still looking at me. I had the impression that it was equally as startled as I was. When it finally moved, it darted across the room at terrific pace, vanishing into the shadows at the far end of the room. I followed but could find no trace of the thing nor any physical means by which it could have made its exit.

When I had opened the door there had been no more than six feet dividing us. The light was moderately good; certainly good enough to see every feature of a person quite clearly. I believe myself to be a careful observer. For instance, I have taken an interest in bird watching and during the war had some skill in aircraft recognition. I am quite certain that I was not deceived by a trick of light or by my imagination.

Then what was it that I saw? It has since occurred to me that it was not unlike some of the representations of the Egyptian god Horus. Similar beaked creatures may be traced in the folklore of many primitive peoples. Could it have been some form of elemental spirit which was more common in the ancient world? It is a question which I cannot answer except to say that I suspect it to have been the poltergeist, one of those michievious sprites so well authenticated in the annals of psychical research.

My interest in ghosts and hauntings dates from my early teens. Even today I find it difficult to resist a 'ghost hunt'. On the whole I have been fairly lucky at being in the right place at the right time.

A question that must be asked is, if the observer were not present would the ghost be there? Certainly, my being a natural psychic must have helped: but on a number of occasions other people have been with me and have seen or heard the same phenomenon at the same time as myself.

I have told the story of my first 'ghost hunt' in my book *An Outline of Spiritual Healing* but, as it played an important part in the development of my psychic life, I make no apologies for repeating it briefly here.

Shortly after my mother's death I was sent, as I have described, to Berkhamsted, an old boarding school in Hertfordshire, which dates back to the dissolution of the monasteries. As was natural in such a place, it was steeped in tradition and history.

Once, I remember, I was invited to join a midnight expedition to the boot-room where, legend insisted, an outraged house-master had dismembered a boy's body with a boot knife — needless to say, the story had no foundation in fact.

We crept through dark stone corridors of School House, half in fear of ghosts but far more in fear of the more tangible danger associated with the resident house-master. Eventually we reached our destination, where the boy who had suggested the enterprise insisted that we sit round in a circle with the lights out. He had told us that his mother was a Spiritualist and that he was fully competent to 'summon up the dead.'

We joined hands, sitting on the floor and shivering — half with apprehension and half with cold. Every few minutes the boy who had appointed himself Master of Ceremonies punctuated the proceedings with a sepulchral, "Is anybody there?" A small gasp of relief could be heard when there was no answer.

After a while we all became bored and started to lark

about and make the sort of noise that we considered a ghost should make if it were capable of making a noise. While this was going on I became aware in the half light that one of the younger boys was staring fixedly into a corner of the room. I followed his eyes and saw a middle-aged woman, dressed in a brown frock coming down to her ankles. Her face was very yellow and she seemed to be smiling faintly in my direction.

None of the other boys seemed to be able to see her but they suddenly became very quiet and the atmosphere of the room appeared to be charged with an electric apprehension.

There was a very loud bang on the door of the boot room. For a moment there was a frozen silence. No one enquired "Who did that?" or "What was that?" Our only idea was to get back to the safety of the dormitory as quickly as our legs would carry us. Not surprisingly, there was little bragging about this episode in the morning and the majority of the participants seemed to want to keep it as quiet as possible.

I saw the woman in brown many times after this. It seemed as if she were searching for something around the corridors. I remember this woman particularly as she was the first 'spirit form' I was to hear speak.

For some days I had been trying to fight off a severe summer cold as I wanted to play cricket for my House on the following Saturday, and it was the first time I had been chosen for the team. During a French lesson matters came to a head when it was noticed that I was shivering and flushed. I was sent to the school matron to be appropriately dosed and sent to bed. My condition not being serious enough for me to be sent to the school sanatorium I was promptly despatched to my own dormitory.

The dormitories at Berkhamsted were divided into cubicles and at the foot of each bed there was a clothing cupboard and a wooden chair. Almost as soon as I got into bed I must have fallen into a feverish sleep. When I woke it was early evening. Although the room was perfectly light, shadows had started to form where the curtain at the end of the cubicle shut out the light from the window. Sitting on the chair was the woman in brown. I was terrified at her closeness and I said loudly:

"Go away or I'll shout out!"

She got up and walked to the side of the bed and leaned over me. I could smell a musty, sickly odour coming from her. Then she spoke to me.

"You've got no right to look at me . . . You've got no right!"

I felt so frightened that I dived under the bedclothes and it must have been some minutes before I dared to look out again. She had gone, but the smell lingered in the cubicle for some hours afterwards.

I later heard a theory that this woman had been a former matron, accused of allowing a boy to die through neglect. I was never able to get confirmation of this story. Judging by her mode of dress, the incident, if it had in fact occurred, would have belonged to the early Victorian era.

Berkhamsted, in common with most public schools of that period, had a very active Officers' Training Corps. This preparation for the armed services was, in theory at least, quite voluntary. In fact every boy had three options — the Boy Scouts, the Pioneers or the O.T.C.

The 'Pioneers' was a euphemism for cleaning the school grounds and generally labouring — if there was a lot to be done, at least it passed the time away; but usually what was entailed was standing beside a wheelbarrow, sweating or shivering according to the season.

The Boy Scouts seemed to attract hearty do-gooders who were forever trotting about with flurries of whistles and staffs at the ready. Thus I drifted into the O.T.C. as the least of three evils.

On Fridays, we would have classes in the mornings as

usual, and then the afternoons would be devoted entirely to O.T.C. affairs. This meant that we had to wear our uniforms for the whole day.

How I hated those uniforms. They were modelled on those of a First World War Infantryman. Lashings of brass buttons, baggy breeches and puttees. There must be a way of rolling on puttees so that they remain in position. Mine had a way of perpetually collapsing into a concertina about my boots.

In short, I did not like the O.T.C. A fellow-sufferer was a boy called David Hocken. We teamed up to beat the system, and in general we were pretty successful.

We discovered that the best means of defence was attack. From being surly and unwilling recruits we transformed ourselves into wild enthusiasts. We volunteered for everything — and always managed to muck it up. As Officer's runner, I would trip over my trailing puttees and usually contrive to bring at least one other man down with me.

David's favourite ploy was to affect a slight deafness. He carried garbled messages from sergeant to sergeant, confused map references and directed platoons to impossible places.

Somehow, he managed to appear the least military creature ever created. His bony wrists protruded a good six inches from the sleeves of his ill-fitting tunic. He had a very white face with a pointed nose and one or two clumps of fine whiskers presaging his approaching manhood. Alas, he was destined never to attain it.

On one particularly unpleasant Friday afternoon, when the O.T.C had everyone crawling all over Berkhamsted Common on what the enthusiasts referred to as 'manoeuvres', Hocken and I volunteered to be 'snipers'. On the basis of sheer nuisance value we were detached from the rest of the platoon with instructions to "harry the enemy with delaying fire". As we had been issued with only two blank cartridges between us and neither of our ancient rifles possessed a firing pin, the order was at best a pious hope.

114

The gutted remains of a burnt-out house stood quite close by. This was off-bounds to all boys: the rotting floors and walls presented a very real risk to anyone climbing about on them. With luck we hoped to spend the rest of the afternoon there without being disturbed by O.T.C. enthusiasts.

David was a very intelligent boy, being particularly good at maths and science. Our friendship was based on a shared interest in radio construction, and a mutual disrespect for the more pompous aspects of Public School life.

At first it amused us to pretend that we really were 'snipers'. We took up positions — clambering as high as possible among the charred rafters of the house. Once, a small group of the 'enemy' rested within a few yards of us. In bated whispers we discussed taking them prisoners or alternatively surrendering ourselves to them. We finally decided to leave well alone. One never knew with the O.T.C. when precipitate action might not involve one in a route march or some other such absurdity.

Eventually they left, blundering through the bracken like a herd of elephants. Their departure left us in high spirits. David, who was not normally an athletic boy, showed off his prowess as a tightrope walker along the beams. They creaked and groaned ominously.

"Pack it up, Hocken," I called. "If you fall there'll be the devil of a row!"

The remains of an upstairs floor partly broke his fall; but he landed with a sickening thud without so much as a cry. When I reached him seconds later he seemed to be quite unconscious.

I was in a quandary. Should I leave him and seek help? The road was at least a mile away, and even then it might be ages before a car came by. But maybe he would be all right soon. This was what really held me back. Supposing Hocken did not need help and I went and confessed to where we had spent the afternoon? I decided to see what would happen.

115

David was breathing deeply and evenly, as if asleep. I propped him into as comfortable a position as possible and was relieved to find no obvious indication of broken bones. I squatted beside his prostrate form for what seemed like hours, but which in fact was probably between three and five minutes.

Suddenly, eyes still closed, Hocken jerked upright into a sitting position.

"Steady, old chap," I said, "you've had a fall. Do you feel any pain anywhere?"

Hocken's body started to jerk and twitch. He totally ignored my presence. I am certain that he was still unconscious. He started to speak in a flat, dead voice in a language that I could not understand. It might have been gibberish; but it sounded well formed, as if conforming to some syntax.

He stopped speaking and became very still. I noticed that his legs were crossed in what seemed to me an alarming position. I wondered again if any bones were broken. His features lost their pinched, pointed appearance, for a moment seeming almost round and oriental. He placed his hands together and bowed.

"My brother will return to his home. It will be soon. There is a purpose — always there is a purpose."

David subsided to the charcoal-strewn floor and groaned.

"What happened? I thought I was dead."

"You silly coon, what did you carry on like that for? You had me worried sick," I said.

He blinked.

"I've lost my specs somewhere." He struggled to his feet. "Do you know, I thought I was dead?" he reiterated in a puzzled manner.

I decided to play along.

"In that case you can tell me what it's like to be dead."

Hocken thought for a moment.

116

"Do you know, I can't remember . . . But I'll tell you what. There's a hell of a nasty stink."

David Hocken committed suicide a year later by attaching the tube from a Bunsen burner to the gas and passing it under his bedclothes. Chemistry had always been his best subject.

It is impossible to tell at this juncture whether David was putting on a 'good show' to give me a scare, or whether the fall released some psychic faculty which had been previously latent. The change of features and apparently prophetic message fit in completely with trance mediumship as demonstrated by Spiritualism today — although I was not to realise this until many years later.

The 'burnt out' house was itself an uncanny enough place. It had a brooding atmosphere in which one tended to talk in hushed whispers.

It seems that certain places are more conducive than others to psychic phenomena. For a couple of years I was lent a small cottage in the grounds of a medieval manor house near Saltwood in Kent.

The whole place was steeped in history. The stream that served as a boundary on one side of the house was called Slaybrook after a battle fought there against invading Romans. Higher up it became 'Redbrook' where, it was said, the blood from the battle had turned the water to crimson.

The manor house itself crouched in a hollow. It was claimed that the four knights riding to murder Thomas à Beckett had tied their horses to the four beams outside the house.

The elderly gentleman who was its occupant had seen ghosts on several occasions. They all seemed benevolent, as he was, although one bedroom had a less happy atmosphere and was seldom occupied.

Shortly before I was lent the cottage there had been a considerable ghost 'scare'. A group of teenagers making their way from Sandling railway station to Saltwood village — a journey which took them directly past the manor house — had been severely frightened by something they saw on the road in front of them.

They described it as grey and misty with lumbering movements. Their story might have been dismissed had it not been for the very real fright of the youngsters. An enterprising newspaper reporter checked up on past records and discovered that 'monster' stories had been associated with the spot for more than a hundred years. His story brought in the TV and an attendant horde of sightseers.

By the time I arrived at the cottage the furore had died down. I would have liked to have been able to mount a full-scale 'ghost hunt', but for fear of disturbing the old man, contented myself with lone nocturnal visits to the site of the haunting. Although I never saw anything unusual, there was an atmosphere of fear that caused one to want to turn tail and flee.

One very still winter's night I was awakened by what sounded like a crowd of people in the distance. I pulled on a pair of trousers and a thick pullover and made my way down to the road.

The sounds grew increasingly distinct: feet marching, metal bouncing against metal, horses and wagons. I am convinced that what I heard that night was a Roman legion on the march. It came so close to me that at one point I seemed to be right in its midst.

When, the following day, I told the old man about this, he was not in the least surprised.

"Oh, yes. Several people have heard that. My daughter often does. It's the Romans, you know."

I find it difficult to believe that a group of 'dead' Roman legionnaires were destined to spend eternity marching up and down Kent to no obvious purpose.

Many scenes of hauntings have more than one ghost, as does Slaybrook. In some instances the hauntings need not even concern a person who has died: violent release of psychic energy may be sufficient to trigger off the phenomenon.

When I was in the RAF, I was posted for a short time to Weeton in Lancasire. We lived in wooden huts, some of which also served as stores. It was decided to empty a hut which had been a blanket store and prepare it to be occupied by a fresh intake of airmen. The hut was duly emptied and furnished with neat lines of beds and lockers.

The following morning the place was a shambles: beds, mattresses and lockers strewn everywhere. After an abortive attempt to find the culprits, a fatigue squad was put to the task of restoring it to its former state of military order.

The next day it was again a shambles. For the last time it was tidied and that night guards were posted on both front and rear exits. I know that they remained at their posts and that even during the changes of the guard the hut was never left, as it was my duty to check on this: but in the morning it was in a worse mess than ever. The guards were closely questioned but they had neither heard nor seen anything untoward.

The Flight Sergeant responsible for the fatigue party was an Irishman and a realist about such matters.

"I think we'll put them in another hut, Sir," he said. "It will be less trouble all round, and 'he' doesn't seem to mind the blankets at all."

"But who is 'he', Chiefy?" I asked. "Do you mean to say you know who is doing it?"

"There was a corporal who went mad. He was locked in that hut for a couple of nights and smashed the place to smithereens."

"And then he died?"

"Not at all! He got his discharge and was put into a mental hospital close to his home."

The Flight Sergeant accepted the phenomenon without

further question. It seemed natural to him that the psychic energy of a mentally disturbed person should linger at the site of its release. For that matter he viewed mental illness with the same superstition with which he regarded the 'little people'.

After my first few years as a healer I realised that little or nothing was known about the nature of psychic energy. My past experience of hauntings and continued fascination with 'ghost hunting' made me determined to make the fullest possible use of the opportunities which my training and gifts made available to me.

Chapter XIV

I had come a long way since my first visits to the Kings Cross Spiritualist church. Two years' hard work in my South West London Sanctuary had caused me to be absolutely swamped with patients. The number of healers working with me had increased to over twenty and the clinics in the Co-operative Hall in North London were packed.

An active research group was established in conjunction with my work as well as a special training scheme for young people who wished to develop their healing potential.

Spiritualists are forever talking about something they describe as the 'movement'. This means the whole gamut of organised and disorganised Spiritualist societies — these have been described in so many different books and articles that it seems pointless to refer to them further here. Suffice it to say that I had become a part of that 'movement' — if a rebellious and uncomfortably critical part.

There was no point at which I had said in effect: "I am now convinced of spirit communication through mediums, and that when such messages are transmitted they indicate an evolving state of individual post-mortal consciousness. I am convinced that this provides a basis for a form of worship and thus becomes my religion." There was no conversion, no sudden moment of light.

In fact, there was much in Spiritualism which I disliked. About that time I was interviewed by a reporter on my views and gave the following reply:

"I think Spiritualism has still got too much superstition. I think we have taken the service of Primitive Methodism and attached clairvoyance to it. I think we have got to get something more vital to attract the new generations. One of the truest forms of worship is the expansion of one's own mind. I don't think we have enough psychic research. There is still a lot to learn."

Spiritualists, although a comparatively small group in terms of world religion, must be one of the most schismatic. There is one organisation which could rival the narrowest 'Christian' sects for the harshness of its dogmatism. Among the largest group of Spiritualists there are many non-Christians who prefer to believe in a Universal deity. Some believe firmly in reincarnation, others reject it just as vehemently.

Like many other Spiritiualists, I was prepared to be identified with the 'movement' for what I believed it might become, rather than for what it was. I believed that it offered new hope for mankind, healing for many who were otherwise incurable, and a whole new vista of scientific discovery.

In my enthusiasm I wanted to tell the world; to tell the sick they might be healed, to tell the bereaved that their loved ones lived on, and, possibly even more important, to remind the Spiritualists of their responsibility as torch-bearers for this knowledge which might shape a new era for mankind.

As ever, the ideal tended to dwindle in the face of the actuality. Most Spiritualists tend to be elderly. The majority go to their Sunday meetings to hear something comforting — preferably short — sing a couple of well known hymns, and then sit back for the clairvoyant messages.

My pioneering zest had to be content for its outlet on the platforms of whatever Spiritualist churches were prepared to book someone as young and inexperienced as myself. Congregations varied between five and fifty people, generally being closer to the former than the latter, and were predominantly female.

"We must band together and make our voices heard. We must proclaim the living truth by the example of our lives.

We are the pioneers, the trail-blazers," I declaimed.

Before me were the five trail-blazers. One slept peacefully, one yawned without bothering to smother it, and the other three looked at me like children promised a pantomime and then taken instead to a Greek tragedy.

"May we have the clairvoyance now?" their eyes pleaded.

Demonstrations of clairvoyance have an element of Bingo about them. The time allocated to the medium only allows her to give between five and ten messages — according to their length. This means that the majority of those present must content themselves with listening to what the spirits have to say to others. If this is of a highly personal nature, it adds a little spice: but it is not like receiving a message of one's own.

Consciously or unconsciously, mediums develop highly individual platform styles. There is the slow, deliberate type who explains before she starts that "all my messages are 'spiritual' rather than 'evidential'." This presages a very dull evening.

One of the most popular at that time was a Jewish medium who combined the wit of a cockney Music Hall comedian with the shrewdness of a market salesman.

"I've got your mother with you," he would say. "My life! But she was a beautiful woman." Then, turning to address the rest of the audience: "I should have a message like that. If I should have my mother beside me like that, what it would mean to me!"

I have twice seen him perform remarkable feats of mental mediumship. On the first occasion, we shared a platform at Seven Kings in Essex. I spoke for about thirty minutes or so before he demonstrated clairvoyance.

At the end of the meeting a young reporter from the local press expressed extreme scepticism.

"If your guide knows so much, ask him how much money I've got in my right hand trouser pocket."

123

"Fourteen shillings and eightpence," the medium answered without hesitation. "Wait a minute and I'll tell you what the coins are. Three half crowns, two shillings, four sixpences, four threepenny pieces, a two shilling piece, a penny and two halfpennies."

The reporter pulled out the coins and they were just as the medium had said. He walked away a very shaken young man. The medium called after him:

"Do you want to know the dates?"

"That shook him," I said.

He winked. "Not half as much as it shook me, mate."

Once, when he was demonstrating his gifts in the Co-operative Hall in Holloway, North London, he asked if anyone there knew a man who had been killed in a road accident the previous day. Nobody responded. There was a full minute's silence. The medium addressed a steward at the back of the Hall.

"I want you to go out of the Hall, turn left, and then take the second left and first right. You'll see a man dressed in overalls and a cap, standing looking at a poster advertising this meeting. He's uncertain whether or not to come. Ask him to return here with you."

There was a tense silence while everyone waited with bated breath. At last the steward returned with the man dressed just as the medium had described.

"You were involved in a road accident yesterday?"

"No." The man seemed puzzled.

"Yes, you were. You 'phoned for an ambulance for a man who had been knocked down by a car, and then went round to see his wife as he had asked you to."

"Oh, that! Yes, that's true."

"Well, that man died, but he's standing here beside me now saying 'thank you'. By the way, when you were looking at that poster, were you deciding whether or not to come to the meeting?"

"Yes."

"What did you decide?"

"That it was a waste of time."

"Do you still think so?"

The expression on the man's face was eloquent answer enough. If this incident were a 'put-up' job, then it was an elaborate hoax which was brilliantly enacted. At the time I believed the incident to be absolutely genuine, and retrospectively see no reason to change that opinion.

These demonstrations were not without their hilarious moments.

"I'm coming to you, my dear," said the ultra-spiritual medium. "Is it your birthday?"

The recipient of the message, a lady of somewhat forbidding aspect, agreed that this was the case.

"And you have a husband in the world of spirit?"

"Yes."

"He's here with us now, standing beside you, and holding out a beautiful bunch of red roses — 'For her birthday' — he's saying."

The lady of forbidding aspect was on her feet — neck and face a flaming scarlet — quivering with emotion.

"Well, you can tell him from me to keep his bloody roses. He never remembered my birthday when he was here and he needn't bother now!"

I continued to travel the country giving lectures and demonstrations of healing. Such meetings attracted a small percentage of newcomers, but those attending were mainly ardent Spiritualists. As my reputation grew, so the same people followed me around from place to place.

I became increasingly dissatisfied with this and determined to find some way round it. One of the least pleasant aspects of these meetings was that although I only accepted travelling expenses for my services, the organisers often used the occasion as an opportunity for fund-raising.

Harry Edwards, who had been healing for some years before I came on the scene, was particularly vulnerable to being used in this way, although a collection was usually taken up to further his work. He was an excellent showman and an impressive healer. I always felt that his tendency to overcrowd the platform with helpers detracted from the simplicity of the meeting.

The impending report of the Archbishop's Commission on healing, and growing public interest, convinced me that the time was ripe to launch a campaign which would bring healing to people for whom it was something quite new. Slowly I was formulating a plan. If I had realised at the time the almost insurmountable difficulties involved, I would have quailed at the prospect — as it was, I was young enough to look on it as an exciting adventure.

I bought the largest map of London I could find and pinned it up in my office. It occupied one entire wall. There was no doubt about it, London was a big place.

Chapter XV

I called it the 'All-London Healing Campaign'. It took a
year's hard preparation. The membership of the Fellowship
of Healing was temporarily built up to fifty. They were all
volunteers who gave their precious spare time while working
for their living during the day.

Teams were trained to staff information desks and indi-
viduals appointed to take over tasks for which their normal
jobs specially fitted them.

I wanted to reach the ordinary public and to do so I was
willing to go out to them rather than wait for them to come
to me.

Psychic News (the world's most widely read Spiritualist
newspaper) welcomed the campaign with banner headlines.

"BIGGEST-EVER HEALING CAMPAIGN — IT WILL
REACH EVERY LONDON HOUSEHOLD

"There are 28 boroughs in the Great Metro-
politan Area. Each in turn will be the scene
of a propaganda healing meeting held at the
Town Hall.

"Features of the Campaign will include
leaflets distributed to every house in the
borough — 10,000, 15,000 or more according
to the population of the area.

"100 posters advertising each meeting on
prominent local sites.

"Advertising in the local press.

"Free admission to every meeting."

In heavy black type it was added:

"THIS IS THE MOST INTENSIVE AND COMPREHENSIVE DRIVE TO PUT HEALING ON THE MAP THAT HAS EVER BEEN ATTEMPTED. AFTER LONDON IT IS INTENDED THAT THE REST OF THE COUNTRY SHALL BE COVERED IN THE SAME WAY."

The first meeting was planned for October 25th, 1956. Posters and circulars were duly printed, together with a longer leaflet with more detailed information on healing and an address where further information could be obtained.

Two weeks prior to the meeting our posters were pasted on the hoardings. Six full-size fourteen-sheet displays and one hundred smaller ones. As I drove round the district inspecting them, it was hard to realise they had anything to do with me.

Our fifty circularisers were due to meet at my South London house at 10 a.m. on the two Sunday mornings prior to the meeting. One of the helpers had made fifty bags to sling over the circularisers' shoulders, and an impressive heap of square packages containing 15,000 handbills stood in my hall. We were all set to go — or so I thought.

A few days before the handbills were due to be distributed, I thought it might be a good idea to take a thousand or so and get the thing started. The system was very simple. Each circulariser was handed an A — Z Guide to London with a section marked off; they pushed their bills through every letter-box and then returned to a pre-arranged rendezvous to pick up more circulars.

It was impossible. I got hopelessly lost, circularised the same street twice and finally gave up in despair. In five and a half hours I had succeeded in delivering a little over two hundred leaflets. At that rate we would be lucky to distribute 5,000 let alone 15,000.

The organisation of circularising had been delegated to Jack Roberts. He was an indefatigable worker. A tall man, with a florid face and a handle-bar moustache, he looked more like a retired Indian Army colonel than the motor trader he in fact was. One great advantage was that his job usually enabled him to lay on sufficient transport to move fifty people from point A to point B.

I telephoned Jack and expressed my worries in very flat tones.

"Leave it to me," said Jack. "I'll come up with something."

And he did! With the help of a young nurse who was part of the team, he drove round every street in the district preparing lists which would enable the circulariser to remain on one side of the road while his partner did the other. The lists followed on perfectly so that no one would get lost and there would be no duplication.

Even so, it was a baptism of fire. It is possible to learn a great deal about human nature on a day's circularising. People who fix a strand of barbed wire along the top of their gate to tear your fingers, dogs which lie in wait to have your hand off as it comes through the letter-box with the handbill, the person who spits on it, screws it up and throws it at you; but to balance all this is the little old lady who says:

"You must be worn out. Come in and have a cup of tea . . . Is that your friend on the other side of the street? Bring him in with you; he'll be tired, too."

We had appointed a Public Relations Officer who attempted to interest the local press in what was going on. It reflects the climate of opinion at the time that many were sneeringly hostile.

The *South London Advertiser* of the week before the

129

meeting, beneath the headline:

"FAITH TRIO OFFER MIRACLE CURE",

wrote a snide story with a picture showing me treating a pekingese. The caption read:

"Gordon Turner, the 32-year-old ex-journalist
who aims to spirit South London's ills away
is willing to right your pet's troubles too."

"FAITH — AND MRS. B. IS CURED IN 4 MINUTES
FLAT",

read their headline after the meeting; but the story beneath it was, if anything, frankly puzzled.

"The pained expression on the dark, lined
face of 43-year-old Jamaican Mrs. Ethlin
Beaumont, of Brixton Hill, broke into a
smile for the first time in 14 months. Life
had returned to her paralysed limbs — and by
a modern miracle, she claimed.

"For months she walked with back arched,
taking small steps because of the arthritis
that paralysed her left side.

"Before 450 people attending a demonstration
of spiritual healing at Lambeth Town Hall
on Thursday, she stood up straight and crossed
the stage with a wide, steady step."

Christopher Evans, now an eminent doctor of psychology, writing the front-page story in *Psychic News* was

130

unashamedly jubilant.

"The demonstration of spiritual healing
given before an audience of 400 at Lambeth
Town Hall on Friday evening may prove to
have been the first step in one of the most
interesting and far-reaching experiments in
the history of modern Spiritualism."

I had deliberately chosen a small hall for our first meeting
— it was important that the morale of the voluntary helpers
should be boosted. But even so, it was possible to find cracks
in my organising.

At the termination of the meeting, the healers were
mobbed, and this resulted in one or two unhappy incidents. I
decided to mark letters on the programmes so that it would
be possible to bring those wishing healing forward in groups
of twenty or thirty.

Our second meeting was at Stoke Newington Assembly
Hall in North London. I knew that this would be a difficult
one. It was a very poor neighbourhood, and it was going to
take a lot to get the people out of their homes and into the
Town Hall.

"A 60-year-old woman, who claimed she had
not walked without a stick for two years,
put down her stick and walked unaided about
the stage of Stoke Newington Assembly Hall
on Monday after she had received treatment
from Spiritual healer Mr. Gordon Turner.

"She was Mrs. R. Jacobs of 2 Tailworth
Street, Whitechapel, who said that she had
suffered from osteo-arthritis for four or
five years, and although she had 'every

131

form of medical treatment' her condition
had not improved.

"Over 600 people attended the demonstration
and at its conclusion nearly 200 stayed in
the Hall to receive treatment from 12 other
spiritual healers,"

wrote the *Hackney Gazette*.

The reporter from the *Stoke Newington Observer* was
more cautious:

"On Tuesday, I and perhaps 500 of the 700
people who passed through the doors of the
Assembly Hall hoped to be either converted
into a believer in spiritual healing or be
convinced that it was just merely an eye-
catching stunt.

"Admittedly — I saw some things there that
would take a great deal of explaining but,
I must confess, I am still not entirely
convinced that what I did see can be explained
only in the words 'spiritual healing'."

This set the pattern that the rest of the campaign was to
follow. Hours of back-breaking circularising; weary helpers
dropping out and others stepping forward to take their
places; crowded Town Halls and sceptical reporters. Always,
there seemed to be the one case which stood out from all the
others.

"64-year-old Mrs. Helen Vandervelde, of
Fairview Road, Tottenham, hobbled up on two

132

sticks to the stage at the Municipal Hall
Tottenham, at a demonstration of spiritual
healing there last week. Mr. Gordon Turner,
one of the most prominent 'healers' in the
country, and his assistant Mr. W. Prince,
gave her treatment, then Mrs. Vandervelde
walked off the stage — slowly, but without
hobbling — and without using her sticks,"

wrote the *Tottenham and Edmonton Weekly Herald*.

Tottenham Town Hall was outstanding for more than those who came on to the platform to be healed. Before the meeting there was a queue outside the Town Hall over two hundred yards long. Eight hundred people were crammed into the Hall and over a hundred more were allowed to stand — even so, a hundred or more people waited outside the Hall for the termination of the meeting so that they might come inside to be healed.

Psychic News ran its story under the headline:

"600 STAYED FOR HEALING AFTER TOTTENHAM'S
BIGGEST MEETING."

It was the fifth demonstration and with it my campaign had really taken off.

Two press reports written at that time bring the demonstrations vividly back to life. John Bowler, writing in the *Kentish Mercury*, headlined his story:

"THE MAN WITH HEALING HANDS WORKED MIRACLES —

"SCEPTICISM GAVE WAY TO AWE.

"A man with no letters after his name, no
brass plate gleaming on his door, no right

133

to be called a doctor, stepped quietly onto
the platform of Lewisham Town Hall on Thursday.
Watched by nearly 1,000 people, he helped to
cure complaints which sufferers claimed have
baffled orthodox medicine for years.

"No instruments were used. He did it all
with his hands. There were no screens, no
theatricalism, and the people 'cured' came
through faith alone.

"The 'miracle man' was 32-year-old Gordon
Turner, who quit writing seven years ago to
devote his life to spiritual healing. His
assistants were a young married couple, Mr.
and Mrs. W. A. Prince.

"Between them this trio claimed to have brought
comfort to over a thousand people, including
the restoration of sight to a blind woman
and the use of limbs to a paralysed boy.

"This story is no myth — it is a fact. I
watched this — South-East London's first
demonstration of spiritual healing. At first
I was sceptical. After twenty-five minutes
I was completely awe-struck.

"During this time I saw Mr. Turner, using his
hands alone, perform near miracles. Take the
case of Mrs. Clarke of Boundfield Road, Catford.
Before she went to this demonstration she had
suffered two years' torture from rheumatoid
arthritis. Her arms and back were fast becoming
useless.

"After five minutes of Mr. Turner's treatment she was a new woman. To all appearances her complaint had been completely cured. Before leaving the platform she was able to stretch her arms high above her head and cry, 'I didn't feel a thing. It's beautiful. I am a new woman.'

"She was just one of ten cases treated during this demonstration.

"Others who came claimed to have spent pounds on cures for spinal curvatures, slipped discs, osteo-arthritis and deafness.

"Eight cases left the platform almost completely cured. Unsuccessful were two deaf cases, an elderly man and woman. But even they admitted they could hear when Mr. Turner and his assistants touched their ears.

"Slipped disc sufferer Mr. Sidney White of Verdant Lane, Catford, was one of the lucky ones. Before treatment he limped gloomily on the platform and told the audience that he felt like an old man. 'Because of my slipped disc my best companion in bed is my hot water bottle,' he said.

"After treatment he was able to bend down, touch his toes and say he was completely cured and was going out to have a pint to celebrate.

"Mr. Turner's and his assistants' only reward

for the near miracles they performed was a
collection taken during the demonstration
and the tears of joy which welled into the
eyes of many of the people he treated."

The *Kentish Mercury* was one of several local papers to
follow up the cases after a couple of weeks had elapsed. They
wrote:

"It was a night that two people — and
hundreds more — will long remember. The
night faith healer Gordon Turner stepped
quietly onto the platform of packed
Lewisham Town Hall and brought faith and
hope into countless lives by relieving
complaints that had baffled doctors for
years.

"This week the *Mercury* contacted two people
who were 'healed' at this wonder demonstration
a fortnight ago, to find out if they had in
fact been cured or if their symptoms returned
as the fervour inspired at the meeting wore
off.

"Before his wife persuaded Sidney White to
go to the demonstration of spiritual healing,
he spent three years suffering the in-
conveniences of a slipped disc.

"After 'wonder healer' Gordon Turner touched
him with his hands Sid was able to bend down
and touch his toes. He claimed that his
slipped disc no longer troubled him and that
he was off to have a pint to celebrate his

good fortune.

"That's what Sid told everyone in grateful
tones through a mike at the healing demonstration.
But does he still feel the same way now?

"Said his wife: 'Since his cure Sid has been
full of life. He now goes out for long walks
and romps around with the children on the floor.
He's a new man.' "

After my demonstration at the Walthamstow Assembly
Hall, both local papers featured the story prominently.

"HEALER GORDON TURNER PACKS ASSEMBLY HALL MANY CLAIM RELIEF"

ran the front-page headline of the *Walthamstow Post*. The
Walthamstow Guardian headlined their story:

"CRIPPLED MAN (78) WALKS AGAIN AFTER SIX YEARS

Their report was typical of the press we were now
receiving:

"A 78-year-old Walthamstow man waved his arms
and jumped up and down on the stage of the
Assembly Hall, Walthamstow, on Thursday evening.
A few minutes before — virtually crippled by
rheumatoid arthritis — he had been assisted
to the rostrum by two white-coated attendants.
Those few minutes had been put to use by
spiritual healer, Gordon Turner, who ran his
hands over Mr. Charles Asals, of 21 Century
Road.

"Slowly, hands that Mr. Asals had been unable
to put behind his head were moved back. . . .
His back, which had been unable to bend, moved
forward. . . . And his legs, bound by the
paralysis, worked normally again.

"Then there was post office sorter, Mr. C.
Hainsworth, of 14 Higham Hill Road, who for
sixteen years had been unable to move his neck
and arms. He had been injured in a road smash
in 1941 and had been semi-paralysed ever since.
Now he moves with almost complete freedom.

" 'I felt no pain as Mr. Turner treated me.
There was a feeling of a ball of warmth inside
me, a feeling of complete goodness. I feel
wonderful,' he told a reporter minutes after
he had been treated.

"Gordon Turner, in front of a packed hall,
called a dozen people to the stage. He scored
successes with nearly every one of them. And
at the end of the meeting organised by the
Fellowship of Spiritual Healing more than two
thirds of the 900 people who had attended stayed
behind to watch Mr. Turner's team of healers
treat the dozens of people who wanted to be
treated for all kinds of ailments, such as
arthritis, slipped discs and deafness."

Gone were the snide headlines we had at first received
from the papers. Now, the majority reacted with uninhibited
enthusiasm.

"AN INCURABLE'S GRIM LIFE CHANGED BY SPIRITUAL HEALER'S TOUCH — RADIANT FACES AT A TOWN HALL DEMONSTRATION" — *Lewisham Journal.*

"HERE'S THE MAN WITH FAITH IN HIS FINGERS"

was the headline of the *South London Press* over a story which was considerably more enthusiastic than the one that we had received for Lambeth.

"600 PEOPLE CHEER AS SPIRITUALIST HEALS"
— *Fulham and Hammersmith News.*

"500 AT FAITH HEALING MEETING"
— *West London Observer.*

"THIS MAN HAS HEALING IN HIS HANDS"
— *London Chronicle.*

"JOURNAL REPORTER'S TESTIMONY OF TREATMENT BY HEALER"
— *Hornsey Journal.*

"MIRACLE CURES REMINISCENT OF LOURDES WERE SEEN AT CHELSEA TOWN HALL"
— *Chelsea Gazette.*

"SHE'S FREE FROM PAIN AFTER SPIRITUAL HEALING MEETING"
— *Acton Gazette.*

If I had achieved nothing else I had broken through the press-barrier. At one hall there were so many people I had to give two demonstrations. One crowd waited patiently outside for an hour and a half. So many came for healing at the

139

termination of the meeting that the hall had to be kept open until after midnight.

All of this had been done entirely on free-will offerings. The costs were astronomical. After seventeen meetings my funds ran out. I had sunk my all into the campaign which had not been subsidised or received any outside financial backing. But what had been done made everything seem worthwhile. In hard statistics — we had circulated 4,982 miles of London streets, reaching over half a million homes. 10,400 people had received healing and many more had been directed to their nearest healing centre. By any standards, it had to be regarded as an outstanding success.

I knew the time was ripe to launch an 'All-England Campaign'; but it meant seeking the aid of churches and societies throughout the country. I realised how apathetic and parochial many of these groups were — but surely after all that had been achieved in London they must want to help.

It was an utter and complete flop. I drove thousands of miles in snow, fog and rain to halls with less than a dozen people in them. I stuck to it for nearly two years: watching the team of helpers I had gathered around me being slowly eroded away. I wore out one car and clocked 54,000 miles on another before I gave in.

I still felt an overwhelming urge to put over what I knew to be true.

"All right," I decided. "If the problem is in the apathy of the societies, then something has to be done to wake them up."

Chapter XVI

Patients have often asked me whether I think it right to spank a naughty child. I usually reply: "I doubt whether it does the child a scrap of good; but it probably makes you feel a lot better."

This might just as well be applied to my own attempts to shake up the various organisations concerned with healing.

I have previously referred to the Spiritualist 'movement'. The one thing it certainly does not do is move! If it has any volition — then it resembles the notorious 'oozlum' bird which, legend has it, eventually disappears in a rather odd style.

The Spiritualist National Union is the largest British Spiritualist organisation. It has several hundred churches within its administration and has the right to appoint ministers, who may conduct marriages or funerals. I started with them.

At first I did not know the rules. Every time I had a good point, I was ruled 'out of order'. But I am a quick learner and soon I was waving 'standing orders' at the chairman and bouncing up and down on 'points of order'.

I bombarded the press with letters and often I was embroiled in two or three controversies at the same time. It did not achieve a thing.

Next, I tried being constructive. I prepared schemes — drawn up in detail — often entailing months of work. They disappeared into the gaping maw of an appropriate sub-committee and were never heard of again.

The 'movement' was amorphous. Just when you seemed to be coming to grips with it, it withdrew and assumed a different form.

At National Conferences, hours were squandered debating matters totally outside its sphere of influence. Unilateral disarmanent, anti-vivisection, and capital punishment; we sent telegrams to the government which commenced: "This Conference, etc. . . . ," but we never seemed to do anything constructive. It reminded me of the Lobster Quadrille from 'Alice in Wonderland'.

During the period of my campaigns, I had taken a long Sabbatical from the Council of the Healers' Federation. In that time John Britnell had died and Harry Edwards — with outstanding generosity — now housed it, rent free, at his sanctuary in Surrey.

I still retained a seat on the Council, as President of the Surrey and South London Healers' Association. I returned to take issue with Harry Edwards who, in my opinion, had criticised the methods of a fellow healer unfairly. What worried me most was that publicity implied that this was a corporate view of the Federation, rather than the view of one individual.

When I entered the meeting, I was a free rebel: when I left, three hours later, I was chairman-elect and director of an annual healers' Summer School. I wonder if a bird realises what is happening when it has its wings clipped? I did not even notice the scissors!

There were already differences and factions within the Council of the Healers' Federation before I returned to take an active part — but I have no doubt that these increased because of my presence. Enterprises were supported or opposed by some Council members purely on the basis of personality.

In the midst of these undercurrents, Harry Edwards was a lagoon of calm support. I still believe that the rapid growth and development of the Federation stemmed, in large part, from the interaction of our two personalities.

I was bubbling with ideas. He was willing to push towards a desired goal despite all opposition. Without his tenacity, few of my schemes would have got off the ground.

We resolved the 'difference' which had brought me back to the Council by appointing a committee to study various healing methods — particularly in their historical context. This was so much more 'civilised' than attacking individual healers. In fact, when the report was published, it tended to support the views Edwards had previously expressed. He generally had his way in the end!

Our first big success took us both by surprise. I had two driving goals: to bring healing out of the shadow of superstition and to make it readily available to all in need — regardless of race, creed or colour. Where were most sick people? In hospitals, I reasoned. All right, then healers must go into the hospitals and treat them.

I put this before the Federation's annual conference as a proposal that we should contact the various hospital authorities with a view to gaining assent that patients in hospital desiring the help of a healer should be allowed this in the same way as if they had asked for a minister or priest. Conference gave the proposal its overwhelming support.

What I had expected was a massive refusal from the hospitals, giving us the opportunity of fighting the issue in every individual area, thus keeping healing constantly before the public as well as unifying County Associations of healers in a common endeavour. I thought it would take five years to win the battle — in fact, within seven months, two hundred and seventy six hospital authorities, comprising 1,743 hospitals, had agreed to healers treating sick people in their wards, provided that it was with the prior knowledge of the doctor in charge of the case. Seemingly, while the aged watch-dog, the British Medical Association, was watching the front door, we had slipped round the back via the National Health Service.

It did not take a clairvoyant to predict that squalls were on the way. It was essential that we establish our good intent immediately. After all, the Federation had been founded to protect the patient as well as the healer.

We drafted a code of conduct for healers visiting hospitals, and forwarded a copy to the British Medical Council stating that we were willing to amend this at their suggestions, and asking them to report any healer to us who contravened this code.

The storm broke at the British Medical Association Conference at Torquay. Delegates called for action from their Parliamentary members and requested hospital authorities to withdraw the permission they had granted immediately. This was followed by a leading article in the British Medical Journal urging Derek Walker-Smith, then Health Minister, to take action in the matter.

Incredibly, only a couple of hundred hospitals complied with the request — leaving over fifteen hundred permitting healers' visits — and when the Health Minister was questioned in the House, he refused to act in a matter which he considered to be the province of local hospital authorities.

It was quite a victory! I debated the question on TV with Heber Langston, a charming surgeon who knew nothing whatsoever about spiritual healing. He said that if a patient wanted healing, he should leave hospital. Daniel Farson, who was chairing the debate, took issue with the poor man. All in all, he had a rough time, which I did not think he wholly deserved.

There was one aspect of the Federation's growth with which I was less happy. We were sprouting the horrid accoutrements of a provincial social club: banners, car stickers, badges for white coats and lapel badges. Hearing that the debate was to take place, a member of the Council turned up at the studio with the banner and the lot. We won the debate; but it might have been achieved with a lot more dignity.

144

This was my first experience of appearing on television. At the best of times I am unphotogenic. The picture which appeared in a paper was from a photograph taken from the TV screen at the time of the programme. I looked desperately forbidding. Some wag cut it out and sent it to me over a caption cut from a laxative advert: ". . . But since he's been 'regular' his temper's been wonderful."

That year I was presented with a Fellowship Award in recognition of 'services to the science and art of spiriutal healing', at a meeting held in the Royal Festival Hall. One of only five such awards ever made. That same year saw the first of the annual Summer Schools which I directed for the Federation for the next nine years.

I had never organised a Summer School before — come to that I had never attended one: it might have helped if I had known what people did at them.

The venue of the first was London. The Council had specified that there must be at least a hundred members wishing to attend. There were a hundred and twelve. I borrowed the lecture hall of the Spiritualist Association of Great Britain in Belgrave Square, and arranged with them that their canteen would cater for the vegetarians. The remainder went for lunch to a self-service restaurant nearby and we paid the bill each day on the basis of the number of meals consumed.

There were eighteen vegetarians, which left ninety-four carnivores. When the bill for the first day's lunch came in it was for a hundred and six people: the next day it was for a hundred and thirty five: on the third day I went down myself. On to the back of our queue of students had latched half the down-and-outs in London! I was all for the feeding of the five thousand, but not on the narrow budget which the Federation had allotted to me. I still had a lot to learn.

I put students in moderately priced hotels close to Victoria. We were catering at such a low cost that frequently accommodation had to be shared. Most people specified a friend with whom they would be happy to be billetted; but with the remainder I just had to do the best I could.

I thought people might like to meet others from a long distance from their home, and on this bright assumption paired up A. Burn from Ayrshire, Scotland, with C. Draper from Worthing, Sussex.

On the first day I was sitting at the reception desk when a huge lady, dressed in tweeds, walked up and towered over me.

"Would you be Mr. Turner?"

"Yes."

"I've been to my hotel and it's verra nice."

"I'm so glad."

There had been some trouble over the hotels as the main one we were using had been burnt to the ground the previous evening.

"My name is Alys Burn — Miss Burn — from Ayrshire, you remember?"

"Yes, of course. Nice to meet you." The penny still did not drop.

"Well, I want you to know, Mr. Turner, that there's nothing personal in this. I'm sure that Mr. Draper's a verra nice man and a verra guid healer — but if ye dinna mind, I'd rather hae a room to myself."

I loved the Summer Schools. The following year we took Oriel and Keble Colleges, Oxford, and the numbers attending rose to two hundred and forty one. We then moved to Rustington, Sussex, where we were to stay for a further seven years. Attendances topped three hundred and fifty and people travelled from all over the world to be present.

How different these gatherings of healers were from the stormy council meetings of the Federation. Every healer who attended gave something of himself. Two that I shall always remember were Lolli and Willi.

146

Lolli hailed from southern India and taught yoga. Willi was from Holland. Although based so far apart, they were able to maintain contact with each other through meditation links. It was in this way that they 'sensed' the Summer School and travelled to England to participate.

During the absent healing session on the last night of the Summer School, Willi asked if he might say a few words.

"I see us," he said, "as pearls, in a necklace that circles the earth. Each pearl on its own is beautiful and adds to the beauty of the necklace. But no one pearl may be perfect — only the necklace may attain that. Now we have become that necklace we shall remain each a part of each other — despite distance, despite time, despite death."

I was impressed by the elderly people who came to the Schools and kept up with the entire strenuous programme. At every School there were a number of healing cures. Occasionally, there were lighter moments, too.

One morning I was wakened at 7 a.m. by a lady who was breathing heavily as if she had been hurrying.

"Mr. Turner?"

"Yes."

"My friend has been rather a long time in the bathroom."

I thought that she was looking for alternative facilities and started to direct her.

"She's been in there over an hour, and she doesn't answer when I bang on the door."

I hurried over to her wing of the camp: pausing only to collect a lady doctor who also happened to be a healer. I tapped only once on the door. When there was no reply I hit it with my shoulder with my full fifteen stone behind it. Not only the door, but the entire frame fell inwards, with me on top.

Floating in the bath was a little lady who looked for all the world like a miniature Margaret Rutherford. The doctor pulled the plug out while I hoisted the lady from the bath.

She had swallowed a lot of water: but mercifully was otherwise none the worse for her adventure. As she regained consciousness her only concern was whether I had seen her. Naturally, she was reassured on the point. The doctor told me afterwards that had we been a minute later she would have been past help.

Many years after this incident, I was asked to open a bazaar for a church in Essex. The President of the fund-raising committee was the lady whom I had rescued from her bath.

"Ladies and gentlemen," I began, "I think I have seen more of your lady President than most of those present today."

The joke was a shared secret between us.

A lady who visited the School from Sweden requested an interpreter as she could not speak English. I was at some pains to arrange this; it was therefore a disappointment when, half-way through the School, I saw the interpreter by the swimming pool while the woman sat without help through a lecture.

I later taxed him on it.

"It's quite all right," he said. "She tells me she can follow every word of the lecture just by looking into the speaker's eyes."

I got him to question her on the lecture that afternoon. It was perfectly plain that she knew what it had been about. She could not tell us how, but she could understand. It was, I suppose, a perfect demonstration that where there is love there can be no barriers. This, after all, is what healing is all about.

Matters with the Federation Council had now reached such an all-time low that I dreaded the meetings. In the chair, I used humour time and again to avert head-on rows. It was nothing for such a meeting to last four and a half hours. I seldom slept on the nights prior to or directly succeeding them.

For me at least, the sacrifices were greater than I could long sustain.

Chapter XVII

While I was occupied with the All-England Healing Campaign, the majority of our voluntary helpers had drifted into other enterprises. Four of them went to Jordan to open a home for refugee Arab children; another went to New Zealand to open his own healing sanctuary — I am sure that the experience they had with the Fellowship stood them in good stead in their chosen vocations.

My healing work had grown enormously. People travelled to see me, not only from all over Britain, but from abroad.

A member of the Australian government came to me with a recurrent back problem. He had been troubled with it for more than ten years.

"How long are you here for?" I enquired.

"Just for this appointment," he replied blithely. "You'll fix it."

He returned home cured.

I have found, over the years, that the attitude of the patient, and those around him, makes a considerable difference to the results of healing treatment.

It is not a matter of 'faith'. Animals and very young children, for instance, make far better patients than most adult people.

The patient I still dread is the one who starts by giving me an exhaustive list of the healers he has previously visited without success. You are left in little doubt that your name will shortly be added to the list.

The emphasis in my healing had gradually been changing. Where, in the early days, I had liked the sanctuary packed with patients watching one another as they received treatment, I found that I could achieve better results seeing each person privately.

Often, there were deeper problems that one sensed and gently helped the patient unburden. Such a case was Mary.

She was about twenty-five and lived with her mother by adoption on a small-holding. Her hands were rough and work-hardened and her face was coarsened by wind and weather.

Her mother had insisted that she come to see me. She had been bilious and listless for several weeks. The moment I put my hands on her shoulders to attune with her I knew that she was pregnant. I determined to wait for her to tell me.

Mary remained morosely silent throughout the treatment and when I had finished, she rose to leave without a word.

"Give me your handbag."

She looked at me as if I had suddenly taken leave of my senses.

I took it from her hands and removed a full bottle of sleeping pills. She had been planning to kill herself rather than tell her mother of her plight.

As we talked it over, she gradually came to see that things were not quite as black as they had seemed. I helped her break the news at home, and to her amazement she found, instead of recrimination, loving support. Healing can involve more than just the 'laying on of hands'.

I closed down the North London clinic and replaced it with an open 'session' at the Spiritualist Association of Great Britain in Belgrave Square. This move was not favourably received by those working with me, but I needed somewhere more central to see patients and this seemed an ideal situation. Another problem was that the lease on my South London sanctuary was shortly going to expire.

Now, every spare moment when I was not healing was devoted to my numerous committee activities. It was not long before my health began to suffer. I was permanently tired and had to force myself to carry on. I decided to go away on my own and give myself a chance to recoup some of my energies. I decided to set off into the blue without making any plans.

Everyone knows the dream English pub, thatched and standing beside a gently flowing chalk stream. A genial Mine Host welcomes you at the door whilst the smell of his wife's excellent cooking drifts out from the kitchen.

That is what I set out to find. It was early spring and very little was open. I lunched at a thatched pub, not unlike the dream, but with a rapacious landlord and cooking which excelled only in price.

I finally lost heart and finished up in Brighton. It was while I was there that I received a telephone call telling me that there was a house to rent in Eastbourne on a short lease, and that the owners would be happy for it to be used for healing.

My work was in London, but what was to be lost by looking? I drove over to Eastbourne on a gorgeous spring afternoon. The first buds were opening: the birds were singing – "A man must be mad," I thought, "to live in London."

It was a white house shut in by a hedge of bay trees. It had partial central heating, three large reception rooms, three bathrooms and seven bedrooms. The immense kitchen boasted a butler's pantry as well as a roomy scullery. There was a mature walled garden with sixty fruit trees.

The gardener would be happy to stay on, I was told. In fact, it would be a condition of tenancy. I thanked the owners cordially for showing me round and promised to let them have a decision within fourteen days.

"By the way," one of them said as I was leaving. "You will give the gardener a rise, won't you? He's not had a rise in salary all the time we've been here."

"Of course," I promised airily, my head spinning with ideas and plans.

By the next morning I was coming down to earth. The place had not been redecorated in years. There were several walls where fresh damp marks showed ominously. The rent was twice what I had been paying, and the rates were three times as much.

If we moved, five of us would be involved in the new sanctuary. We took a democratic decision from which I abstained.

Packing up to move was a mammoth task. Not only were there the sanctuary records, but all the files and documents of the Summer Schools and committees etc. Somehow, it was all done in time.

Of the remainder of the helpers who had worked with me for so long, several decided to heal at my weekly clinic at Belgrave Square, and the rest bade me sad farewells.

Saying goodbye to the patients was even worse. I had had wonderful support from the local people. The market traders used to leave flowers and fruit on my doorstep — it had been hard to walk past their stalls without gifts being pressed upon me.

Even the local 'gangster' was my ardent supporter, after his wife had been healed. He was normally accompanied everywhere he went by two gentlemen who seemingly compensated for what they lacked in intelligence by a superfluity of bulging muscles.

On one occasion, I am told, my work was being discussed in a local pub. The 'gangster' was relating the story of his wife's healing when a foolhardy know-all interrupted.

"You don't believe in that rubbish, surely. It's all done by paying people to say they've been healed."

The 'gangster' gave a brief nod to one of his hatchet men. Moments later the sceptic was lifted into the air by two huge fists firmly gripping the lapels of his jacket and was shaken until his teeth rattled like castanets.

"Did you say something?" enquired the 'gangster.'

153

"Er, no . . . ah, er, yes . . . er, I mean yes, I quite agree with you. Yes."

Although I cannot approve the method, it must rate as one of the most rapid conversions on record!

Over the years I have treated members of five Royal families, and dignitaries from every branch of the Establishment. Healing does not work any the more readily for the great than it does for the humble.

Because the majority of my patients come to me by word-of-mouth recommendation, there is a tendency for one to see people in specialised groups. At one time I was treating two Cabinet Ministers and three Members of Parliament; on another occasion it was a cross-section of the racing fraternity.

My father, who is passionately fond of horse racing, asked me to try to get a few tips. They always lost. The only time I was able to give him a winner was when a clergyman I was treating confessed to me that he had an infallible horse racing system. After that, he gave me a tip every time he saw me, but he never repeated his initial success.

The house at Eastbourne never got off the ground. From the first it was a nightmare. I waged a continual battle with the damp; but never succeeded in beating it for more than a few weeks at a time.

To cope with the patients I had left in London, I increased my visits to Belgrave Square to twice a week and opened at Eastbourne on the other three days, trying to keep the weekends free to cope with absent healing letters and committee work.

Eastbourne may be a splendid resort to retire to; but it is no place to open a healing sanctuary. It was not that I was short of patients – on the contrary, they came thick and fast. But it was a totally different type of healing from that to which I had grown accustomed.

Normally, the majority of my patients were very sick

people of all ages. At Eastbourne, it was a matter of soothing the aches and pains of the aged. I would have been the first to admit the value of such work. I was happy to look after these patients at my clinics. But a practice made up almost entirely of such cases — it was too much!

There was another even more disturbing aspect. The free will offerings were terribly poor. It was nothing to work from 10 a.m. to 5 p.m. and find at the end of the day a collection of less than £1. It was not enough to pay the heat and light, let alone the rent.

This was the situation when two of the five people involved decided to quit. Bills came in at a terrifying rate. I sold first my personal possessions, then my car; but still the debts mounted. Not unnaturally, my health started to deteriorate further.

It was under this pressure that I finally signed a contract to heal virtually full time for the Spiritualist Association of Great Britain. Somehow, I had to find the money to pay the debts.

My week's work at Belgrave Square entailed four three-hour clinics, four six-hour sessions of private appointments and running two healers' training groups. If I had been fit when I had started, I might just have managed to sustain it; as it was, the writing was already on the wall.

At first I commuted daily; leaving home at 8 a.m. and returning at about 10 p.m. This was all very well in the summer but in the winter it was hopeless.

The British are unfailingly taken by surprise at every fall of snow. Despite the fact that it has been happening every winter since time immemorial, we still regard every snowfall as a unique phenomenon. In such conditions, my train once took seven hours to travel from Victoria to Eastbourne.

In the end, I found myself a pied-a-terre in Ebury Street, close to Belgrave Square. It consisted of a nasty little green-emulsioned bed-sitter, with a kitchen recess and a bathroom. It cost me slightly less than my weekly fares.

To reach it I had to climb four flights of stairs, and invariably when I reached the top I would be puffing and panting, with a pain like a tight band round my chest.

"I must ease up," I told myself. "I ought to go to a healer."

But my life was moving at such a frenetic pace that there never seemed either the time or the opportunity.

The call upon my services at the Spiritualist Association was immense. Clinics were so busy that I seldom had time to spend more than two or three minutes with any one patient. Private appointments were booked up weeks in advance; but there was always a good reason why I should fit in 'just one more person'.

"But you've only half an hour for your lunch now," a receptionist would protest.

"Never mind. I never eat lunch, anyway."

After a while they just booked patients into my lunch hour automatically. Then it was "we can just fit in one before I take my evening class", and finally, "well, I can easily come half an hour earlier in the morning".

And despite all this the queue of people remained undiminished. If I left my small consulting room to go anywhere else in the building, people would be continuously stopping me.

"Surely, you can spare just five minutes?"

I became obsessed with time. I ran everywhere. If I was not working, I was beset by guilt. There was no way I could switch off. I could not even meditate any more. It was the Cresta run with the toboggan totally out of control.

I would arrive at 10 a.m. and leave at 9 p.m. During this time I rarely had a break of more than fifteen minutes. When I left in the evening I was past food.

Perhaps the worst feature of all this was that I felt terribly lonely. I could not sit alone in my little bed-sitter. At first, I walked the streets or went to a news theatre; finally, I would finish up in a pub for a beer and a sandwich. As my stress increased, so the beer became a whiskey and eventually two or three.

A reporter from the *News of the World* came to see me. I explained that I was so overwhelmed with work that I could not cope with anything further. We had lunch together and he was very persuasive.

"Can you cure cancer?" he asked me as we parted.

I answered cautiously. "There are people still living who came to me with terminal cancer as long as fifteen years ago. But I would be very cautious about making any claims."

They printed a two page article — a complete centre-page spread with plenty of photographs. It stated categorically that I claimed to be able to cure cancer. The result was catastrophic!

Belgrave Square was besieged. At my clinics people fought past my receptionist and pushed their way into my consulting room. Everywhere I went people knew me: in the streets: in shops: in trains: in buses: there seemed no escape.

Letters poured in by the thousand. I took on extra help so that every letter could be answered personally.

One night I was opening these letters in my room in London when the whole weight of it hit me. So many of them were pitifully illiterate, from helpless, lost people: "... I have cancer of the throat and my doctor says ...", "... my baby has leukaemia ...", "... my husband has ...", and always: "... please heal him ...", "... please heal me ..."

I could feel their need and my own inadequacy. Tears poured down my cheeks and I fell upon my knees and prayed as I have never prayed before.

"Dear God! Not me! Free me from this burden!"

Somehow I managed to ride the storm and carry on; but my health was failing and I had to take more and more time off. After each absence the queue had increased yet further.

At the weekends I was now so tired that I could not tackle the problems waiting for me at home. The Federation's demands upon me grew rather than diminished.

Things were going from bad to worse. I started to procrastinate. From sheer exhaustion I neglected the routine jobs my various offices required. Now the contentious element within the Federation Council turned upon me, continuously pushing me for work I had not completed.

Harry Edwards came to my aid. With great generosity, he took me as his guest to the South of France. All day we lay in the sun, and in the evenings we yarned for hours. Inevitably, we turned to discussing our various healing experiences: we found much in common that we had discovered for ourselves. From these conversations we drafted the outline of a study course for healers.

Initially, we intended to put it out under our joint names; but finally decided to donate it to the Healers' Federation.

If I had known at the time the violent antipathy this course was to arouse in certain members of the Healers' Federation Council, I would have had nothing to do with it.

On the last day we went down to the beach to sit in the sun for an hour or two. A plane flew over, and automatically our eyes moved upwards and we felt the 'pull' of home.

"How long is it since you had a holiday?" Harry Edwards asked.

I thought hard. "Twelve years."

"And before that?"

"Seven years."

"You should get away for a break at least twice a year," he said solicitously.

How I wished I could!

When I returned home, the ruins of the Eastbourne venture were nearly cleared up. Jo Prince, the last of the original five, had worked like a slave in my absence, packing and selling the remnants of what had started out with so much hope and enthusiasm.

I rented a flat in Holland Park and continued to work for the Spiritualist Association in Belgrave Square. I was still having frequent bouts of ill health and these caused the reception staff a considerable amount of work in cancelling and re-booking patients. Eventually, I stopped working there and saw such patients as I could cope with in my own flat.

By the time the 1966 Summer School came round, I was far too ill to undertake the rigorous work it entailed.

Medical examinations had revealed a worsening in the condition of my heart, a malignancy of my right kidney was suspected and I had explosively high blood pressure. I was ordered into hospital, but refused to go, at least, not until the Summer School was over. I was determined to go ahead with it.

I think, even then, that I might have got away with it had it not been for the frightful row which was brewing among certain members of the National Federation Council. Most of those involved had to attend the School and this meant a constant atmosphere of tension.

It was my first day's healing after the School and my penultimate patient of the day. He had had a stroke and suffered a considerable loss of movement.

"Are you going to cure me?"

"I'll do my best," I said.

"I could move my right foot after only one visit, and they said that was impossible. When are you going to have me walking again?"

"That may take a little time."

He laughed. "I see. The impossible you do at once, but miracles take a little longer."

I felt a sudden loss of mobility in my left hand. I asked him to excuse me and left the room.

Epilogue

Life is still leasehold. I now accept time by the second rather than by the hour.

To misquote Gertrude Stein: 'A healer is a healer is a healer.'

I am content with that and through it I am fulfilled.

All that remains of my paralysis is a slight loss of dexterity in one hand and a limp on my left side when I am tired. They are but a small inconvenience and serve as a reminder when I attempt to impose my will over such gifts as I have been given.

I do not think I wasted my period of inactivity. Much of the time I spent exploring my sleep-life and simplifying my techniques of meditation. Subsequently, I have been able to apply these methods to the problems of the mentally disturbed, in particular young people addicted to hard drugs.

Unencumbered by time-wasting committees and societies, my work is as busy as it has ever been. I now work alone, holding no open clinics, but seeing every patient privately.

Recently, my work has extended to America. The enthusiasm there is very like the spirit of the Summer Schools I once directed.

Now, when I appear on radio or television, I am able to speak for myself rather than for any 'movement' or organisation . . . and it feels good.

I still believe in the life eternal. I still believe that, on occasions, post-mortal communication through mediums does take place. But what I do not believe is that this constitutes the basis upon which a religion can be founded.

As a healer, I am prepared to worship in any church with any person of any religion. I cannot conceive of a God who is

160

not universal.

One last story has yet to be told.

In October 1969 I was interviewed on a radio news programme. One of their reporters had brought his Staffordshire bull terrier to me with a serious heart condition. After three or four visits it was healed.

As a result of this interview I received a great many letters. One of these was from a young lady named Daphne Boden. She enclosed a picture of Shadow, her grey Arab mare.

Shadow had a torn Achilles tendon. She had been operated on by a brilliant surgeon at Newmarket, after which she had been put out to grass for three months.

She was still very lame and had, in the meantime, developed brucellosis and her wind was going. All in all, the situation looked very black.

The following Sunday, Daphne and her mother picked me up and drove me out to Richmond where Shadow was stabled. On the way they warned me that she was a very spirited pony who did not take kindly to strangers pulling her about.

At the age of twenty-one Shadow had turned as white as snow. She looked like an angel, and that is the way she behaved that morning. I treated her and suggested that for the next fortnight she be walked every day with someone leading her. At the end of this time I would see her again. I said that I hoped she would be completely well in a month.

On my next visit she was so much better that she could be ridden, and within the month she was absolutely sound in wind and limb.

A couple of years later I had dinner with the surgeon who had carried out the operation.

"I'll tell you what I did if you tell me what you did."

"Sorry," I said. "I wish I could; but I just don't know."

Daphne turned out to be a concert harpist and it was not long before I went to one of her recitals. She played

161

beautifully. I sat entranced. She seemed so small beside her big concert harp.

A friendship developed, not only with her, but with her parents who are both brilliant portrait painters.

Daphne worked with me on several projects involving music, including a record on sleep.

Eventually we decided that we would like to get married. It happened so suddenly that it surprised everyone, including Daphne and me.

One of the first people we told was Shadow; but she was not in the least surprised. She had had it planned that way all the time.

As I have said before, life is still leasehold; but every second of it is precious.

82 Addison Road,
Kensington,
London.